THE BIRDMAN OF TREADWELL

Diary of a Treadwell Gold Miner

By Edwin Warren
Presented by Barry Kibler

Bloomington, IN — authorHOUSE® — Milton Keynes, UK

AuthorHouse™
1663 Liberty Drive, Suite 200
Bloomington, IN 47403
www.authorhouse.com
Phone: 1-800-839-8640

AuthorHouse™ UK Ltd.
500 Avebury Boulevard
Central Milton Keynes, MK9 2BE
www.authorhouse.co.uk
Phone: 08001974150

© 2007 By Edwin Warren Presented by Barry Kibler. All rights reserved.

No part of this book may be reproduced, stored in a retrieval system, or transmitted by any means without the written permission of the author.

First published by AuthorHouse 4/25/2007

ISBN: 978-1-4259-6064-3 (sc)

Library of Congress Control Number: 2007902541

Printed in the United States of America
Bloomington, Indiana

This book is printed on acid-free paper.

Dedications

I Dedicate This Book To The Following:

Edwin Warren, the man who wrote it and lived it, Edwin unknowingly preserved a little bit of history for those who followed him in life.

Stanford University, for if it was not for Stanford, Edwin would have never went to Alaska to earn his tuition by working in the Treadwell Gold Mine, where he was nearly killed on several occasions. The price Edwin paid for his tuition was very small compared to what students now pay, but in the terms of sacrifice and hard labor, I would imagine Edwin probably paid as high of a tuition as anyone who ever attended Stanford.

The miners of Treadwell, especially to the two hundred miners who lost their lives, and the many others who were injured working at Treadwell, such as the young Italian who lost his life on his very first night working in the shaft.

The native Indians of Alaska, who added color and charm, as well as character, to the *Treadwell Diaries of a Miner*.

The members of the Christian Endeavors, the Friends' church, for without their friendship and support, Edwin would have probably never returned to Alaska in 1904.

Contents

Dedications v
Notable Entries xi
First Trip 1903: xi
Second Trip (1904): xi
Alaska State Library Digital Archives xiii
Foreword xv
In My Grandfathers Footsteps xv
Introduction xxi
"Diaries Vividly Depict Mining History" xxi
About John Treadwell xxiii
Acknowledgments xxv

Chapter One:

North to Alaska 1
STARTED FOR ALASKA ON MY WHEEL 1
SAN JOSE TO STOCKTON ON MY WHEEL 1
SAN JOSE TO SACRAMENTO ON MY WHEEL 2
SEATTLE TO CLOVERDALE BY TRAIN 3
BIRDS OBSERVED NEAR CLOVERDALE, B.C. 3
BIRD WATCHING 3
CLOVER DALE TO VANCOUVER 4
ABOARD THE STEAMER *PRINCESS MAY* 4
IN THE NARROWS 5
ABOARD THE STEAMER *HUMBOLDT* 5

Chapter Two:

The Treadwell Gold Mine 8
I AM NOW A TREADWELL MINER 8
SUFFERING FROM THE GAS 8
CROW-HOPPING RAVENS 9
BIRD WATCHING 9
A REMARKABLE MAN 9
AUDUBON DONATION 10
THE FIRST ICEBERGS I'VE SEEN 10
I FAINTED FROM THE EFFECTS OF THE GAS 10

vii

LETTER FROM MARGARET WARREN	11
BIRD WATCHING	11
MEN WAITING FOR DINNER	12
FIRST PAYDAY	12
WROTE TO MARGARET	13
SLOVENIAN HOLIDAY	13
THREE KILLED & THREE INJURED	14
NEAR RIOT AT TREADWELL	15
NEAR EXPLOSION AT TREADWELL	15
A RAINY DAY	19
TWO MEN KILLED; MANY NOW QUITTING	19
A WEALTH OF PLEASURE AND INFORMATION	19
DROPPED THE CAGE WITH MEN UNDERWATER	20
CHAPLAIN CLEMMENS	21
RAVENS AND CROWS ON LITTLE JUNEAU ISLAND	22
ONE COULD SEE WONDERFUL THINGS	23
WORKING ON SUNDAYS	23
WORKING WITH A DANGEROUS MAN	24
RAIN SOON	28
ELEMENTS OF GEOLOGY	28
FOGGY DAYS	29
A SCENE OF LIFE AND BEAUTY	29
LAND BIRDS OF MONTEREY	30
PAYDAY	30
THE NOTORIOUS TOUGH, RED NELSON	31
SUNNY DAYS	31
THE TREADWELL GHOST	31
THE CHRISTIAN ENDEAVORS	32
BALD EAGLES SPOTTED TODAY	33
SAN FRANCISCO FIRE DEPARTMENT	33
THE NATIVE MISSION	34
THE BEAR'S NEST BOARDING HOUSE IS COLD	34
THE TREADWELL BAND	35
SNOWFALL	35
ANOTHER MAN KILLED TODAY	35
TREADWELL POST OFFICE	36
BAD WEATHER, GOOD FOOD	36

WINTER IS HERE	36
STILL SNOWING	37
WATER IN THE MINE	37
WHALES SPOUTING	37
CAGE TENDER	37

Chapter Three:

Homeward Bound To Pacific Grove, CA.	39
FAREWELL TO TREADWELL	39
BEAR'S NEST BOARDING HOUSE	40
NATIVE VILLAGE OF PETERSBURG	40
PORT OF KETCHIKAN	41
QUEEN CHARLOTTE SOUND	42
PORT OF SEATTLE	42
ABOARD THE *QUEEN*	43
PORT OF VICTORIA	43
PORT OF SAN FRANCISCO	44
SAN FRANCISCO ACADEMY OF SCIENCE	44
WHEEL STORAGE	45
END OF FIRST TRIP (1903)	45

Chapter Four:

Return to Alaska	46
ABOARD THE *PUEBLO*	*46*
SEASICK	47
BEAUTIFUL WHITE GULLS & ALBATROSSES	47
PORT OF VICTORIA	48
PORT OF SEATTLE	50
SEATTLE	50
THE STATEROOM	51
WE MET THE STEAMER *PORTLAND*	*52*
BOWS AND ARROWS	53
THE FERRY *LONE FISHERMAN*	*55*

Chapter Five:

Return to Treadwell	56
THE THREE HUNDRED STAMP MILL	56
A BEAUTIFUL AFTERNOON	58

A REMINDER OF PACIFIC GROVE 58
HE WAS PRETTY BADLY USED UP 59
FLOCKS OF GULLS ON THE BEACH 60
CHRISTIAN ENDEAVORS, THE FRIENDS' CHURCH 60
THE FRIENDS' CHURCH 62
THE BEAUTY OF INDIAN CANOE 62
RESCUING A LITTLE INDIAN BOY 65
INDIAN BEAR HUNTERS 65
THE DOUGLAS SALOON 67
THE STEAMER *COTTAGE CITY* 69
FINDING FOSSILS ON DOUGLAS ISLAND 70
MONTHLY CLEANUP IN THE MILL 73
NO MORE SUNDAY WORK 74
THE INDIAN CHURCH 75
TAKU HARBOR WITH REV. JACKSON 76
A CANOE FOR THE AFTERLIFE 78
INDIAN BURIAL GROUNDS 79

Chapter Six:

From Treadwell Minor to Stanford Student 81
TONKA INDIAN VILLAGE 81
BELLA BELLA INDIAN VILLAGE 82
PORT OF VANCOUVER 83
PORT OF SEATTLE 83
ABOARD CENTENNIAL 84
ACADEMY OF SCIENCES GALAPAGOS EXPEDITION 88
7 PM: HOME AGAIN PACIFIC GROVE, CALIFORNIA 88
END OF THE SECOND JOURNEY 1904 88

Appendices

The Stanford Years 89
MORE ABOUT THE AUTHOR 93
EDWIN WARREN, THE BIRDMAN OF TREADWELL ... 93
GLOSSARY OF MINING TERMS 95
TREADWELL BENEFITS: 97
ABOUT BARRY KIBLER 99

Notable Entries

{All entries not listed due to large number of entries}

First Trip 1903:

1. April 20, 1903 ………Started for Alaska on my wheel
2. July 29, 1903 ……… I fainted from the effects of the gas
3. August 5, 1903………Three killed and three injured
4. August 6, 1903………Near riot at Treadwell
5. August 17, 1903…….Two men killed; many now quitting
6. August 24, 1903…….Working with a dangerous man
7. September 3, 1903….The notorious tough Red Nelson
8. September 6, 1903….The Treadwell Ghost

Second Trip (1904):

9. April 27, 1904…………Beauty of the Indian canoe
10. April 27, 1904…………Rescuing a little Indian boy
11. April 27, 1904 ………… Indian Bear hunters
12. May 1, 1904 ………… The Douglas Saloon
13. May 4, 1904 …………Finding fossils on Douglas Island
14. May 10, 1904 ………..Taku Harbor with Rev. Jackson
15. May 10, 1904…………A canoe for the afterlife
16. May 19, 1904 ………..Galapagos expedition

Alaska State Library Digital Archives

NOTE: There are many more images of the Treadwell Gold Mine, both while it was an active mine and in its present-day condition. There are also many images of the Native Indians, and the steamships Edwin mentions in his diary, and the Friends Mission.

These images are available on the internet at *http://vilda.alaska.edu* also under Treadwell or Treadwell Gold Mine. Or simply Alaska State Library digital images

(NOTE: Use Image ID# in search.)
Below is a list of images that relate to the *Birdman of Treadwell*
1. General overview of Treadwell - ID# ASL - P87 - 0333
2. Native village of Petersburg – ID# P39- 0674
3. Kasaan Indian Village - ID# ASL - Kasaan - 04
4. Pacific cannery - Taku Harbor -ID# ASL - P-39-0739
5. Indian Grave houses - ID# ASL - P 87 - 0025
6. Friends Mission – ID# ASL - P226 - 414
7. Steamer *City of Seattle* - ID# ASL - P39 - 0363
8. Steamer *City of Portland* - ID# ASL - P39 - 0609
9. Steamer *Cottage City* - ID# UAF - 1994 - 70 -6
10. Steamer *Humboldt* - ID# UAF - 1994 - 70 - 384
11. Steamer *Al - Ki* - ID# ASL - P87 - 1584
(Later shipwrecked as was the *Princess May*)
12. Steamer *Queen* - ID# UAF - 1981 - 192 - 21
13. Beaver Canoe - ID# ASL - P1 - 083
14. Figure Head Indian canoe - ID# ASL - P44 - 03 - 142
15. Bear Hunter - ID# ASL - Funter Bay - 21
16. [Richard] Little Indian boy - ID# UAF - 1994 - 70 - 139
17. Treadwell Club Band - ID# UAA - hmc - 0131
    (Many others images are also available)

Foreword

Presented by Barry Kibler

In My Grandfathers Footsteps

The diaries of my grandfather, Edwin Warren, had been sitting in a drawer for one hundred years. Edwin made two journeys to Alaska, once in 1903, and again in 1904. He worked as a miner at the Treadwell Gold Mine to earn his tuition at Stanford University and to pursue his interest in ornithology. (See the images in appendices titled, "The Stanford Years.")

Edwin kept a diary of the birds he observed in Alaska, as well as the everyday events of a miner working in the Treadwell mine, where he observed and recorded death and injury in the mine all too often. He also recorded in his diary an account of his journeys, which ranged from his bicycle trip from Pacific Grove, California to Sacramento, California, to the various voyages on many different steamships.

I have named Edwin's diaries, *The Birdman of Treadwell,* in my grandfather's honor, as he is the author. The original diaries were written entirely by him in his own hand, sometimes along the way, when riding his wheel, or on rocking steamships, or at the Treadwell mine under stressful conditions. There are actually two diaries, one for 1903 and another for 1904; however, to simplify the title, I refer to them as the diary.

The only changes were to transcribe the diaries into a manuscript. The actual entries are written by Edwin Warren. Edwin took the diaries out of a drawer and passed them on to his daughter, Margaret, on his ninetieth birthday, and she cherished them until near death. At the age of eighty-four, she took them out of a drawer and passed them on to me, Barry Kibler, Edwin's grandson, where they again found a place in a drawer—till the summer of 2003, one hundred years after they were written.

I was unaware of the historical importance of my grandfather's diaries, as was my mother, Margaret, until the summer of 2003. My wife and I were taking a cruise to Alaska and I happened to think of the diaries. I looked the Treadwell Gold Mine up on the Internet to see if I could find out anything about it, if it even existed anymore or if anybody ever even heard of it.

I had the hope that maybe, just maybe, I could locate it and then go there to see the mine, if it was anywhere near where we would be on the cruise ship. The information on the Treadwell Gold Mine was overwhelming; it was across the Gastineau Channel from Juneau, and the cruise ship *Dawn Princess* would be in Juneau for eight hours. I found on the Internet that I could take a city bus from Juneau across the bridge to Douglas Island and the Treadwell complex.

The bus driver was very helpful when I told him I was going to the Treadwell and that my grandfather was a miner there in 1903 and 1904; he told me how to find my way around the Treadwell mine complex. The first thing I saw at Treadwell was the last remaining stamp mill on display, as if it was a monument to the history of the Treadwell Gold Mine—or a giant tombstone honoring those who had met their death at Treadwell.

Up the trail, I ran across the glory hole, a large open pit where gold was first discovered and the mining process began. Which was much like it probably was a hundred years ago. In my mind's eye, I could imagine the native Indians working down in the glory hole, as they were too smart to work underground in the mine (even though Edwin, and others who were college students, did work deep down in the mine). Maybe it was a natural instinct not to work underground that was lost to the white man.

Further down the trail, I ran across the last remaining ore car and could not help but wonder if this was the very ore car that Edwin was leaning on when he fainted from the effects of the gas, while waiting for the skip to take him to the surface.

The next thing I ran across was the skip, a conveyor like machine that took the ore and sometimes the miners to the surface. I realized that this *was* the skip that Edwin was waiting for to take him to the surface when he fainted from the effects of the gas a hundred years ago. I tried to imagine him riding in that skip, like a product in a modern factory. Then I found the old railroad bed, and in my mind's eye, I saw the notoriously tough Red Nelson stumbling along the tracks.

A little further down the trail, I could imagine, in my mind's eye, hearing a lusty squalling coming from a little Indian boy, who had seemed to have fallen through some kind of a platform. Then there it was: the Treadwell dock, out past the sandy beach, created from the tailings from the Treadwell mine. This is where the old steamships came and went, and where Edwin came and went, one hundred years ago—almost to the day.

Then down below me, I could imagine seeing—not in my mind's eye, but in hindsight—a magnificent Indian canoe passing by. A little while later, some Indians in a rowboat passing by represented to me the transition from the traditional Indian ways to the white man's ways captured in Edwin's diaries.

This was more than two small boats passing by; it was a way of life, a simpler way of life, and it was passing by to be lost for all time. I saw the old pipes sticking up in the air, and the remains of the chain link fence from the Treadwell tennis court. I also saw old water pipes and various mining machinery lying about, including many of the old rollers from the vanner room, rusting away.

I could not help but think of the two hundred miners who lost their lives, or the others who were injured at Treadwell. Especially the young Italian Edwin knew who lost his life on his very first night's work in the shaft. This made me realize that, in a way, I also almost "died" in the Treadwell mine even though I was not yet born: If my grandfather had been killed—in the near collision with the ore train, or from the incompetent hoist engineer dropping the cage with volatile explosives—I would never have been born.

As the *Dawn Princess* pulled away from the docks in Juneau, I was glad that I had come here, for now, I shared the memories of a portion of my grandfather's life. As we pulled out of Juneau, the *Dawn Princess* was escorted by a coast guard patrol boat and a zodiac boat that circled the cruise ship. I could not help but notice the anti-aircraft guns on the patrol boat—that's something you never see on a patrol boat of that small size in California.

I wondered if it was due to 9/11, or because of the large number of bush planes in Alaska. As a veteran of the coast guard, it filled me with pride to be an ex-coast guardsman and an American as I watched the coast guard boats circle our ship, like a mother hen protecting her chicks. I could not help but holler out to the sailors on the zodiac "semper paratus!" or "always ready," the coast guard motto. This was not the first time I have been this far north; I was up here forty-five years ago, in 1958, on the U.S. Coast Guard cutter *Minnetonka* on Ocean Station Romeo, between the Aleutian Islands and Siberia on the Bering Sea, sandwiched in between where my father, Lloyd Kibler, was a machine gunner in 1918 on the Trans-Siberian railroad with the U.S. Army in World War I, and where my grandfather, Edwin Warren, was a miner at the Treadwell Gold Mine in 1903 and 1904.

*U.S. Coast Guard patrol boat with
Zodiac boat aboard
Barry Kibler creator*

*U.S. Coast Guard cutter Minnetonka
Kibler collection*

xix

Introduction

"Diaries Vividly Depict Mining History"

By Sarah Hurst, for Mining News SE Alaska

Keen ornithologist from California witnessed tragedies, near misses at Treadwell mines on Douglas Island, at beginning of last century. As all miners know, if you do some digging there's a chance you'll strike it big. Barry Kibler of California dug out his Grandfather's diaries, and found a treasure trove of stories about his stints working at the Treadwell Gold Mines in Douglas, near Juneau, in 1903 – 1904, Kibler, a retired truck driver recently finished transcribing the diaries of Edwin Warren.

Warren himself set out for Alaska by bicycle, train and steamer, hoping to study birds and save money for his tuition at Stanford University. He risked his life in the mines, but survived the experience and lived to the age of 92. There were four mines in the Treadwell complex: Ready Bullion, Mexican, Seven Hundred Foot mine, and Treadwell. By 1917, some ten million tons of ore had been removed from below sea level, and the land in several areas was beginning to subside. Three of the four mines flooded with 3 million tons of sea water on April 21, of that year, and they were closed down.

About John Treadwell

John Treadwell was a carpenter and builder. He also had many years' experience as a miner in California and Nevada before he came to Alaska. John was building a home for a banker in San Francisco, when the news of a gold strike on the Gastineau Channel broke. The banker, John Fry, paid John Treadwell's expenses to Alaska to look into the prospects of investing in gold claims on Douglas Island, across the Gastineau Channel from Juneau. In 1881, John purchased the Paris lode claim on Douglas Island from Pierre Joseph Erussard for the sum of $400. He then proceeded to purchase other claims, and formed a partnership with other investors.

The Treadwell mine complex was the largest gold mine in the world in its time. Three million ounces—or a hundred tons—of gold were mined at Treadwell. Nearly two thousand men worked at Treadwell in its heyday. Approximately two hundred men were killed working at Treadwell, and many others were injured. The towns of Douglas and Juneau existed to service the Treadwell mines. The Treadwell put Juneau on the map. The four mines that made up the Treadwell complex were the Treadwell, Ready Bullion, the Mexican, and the Seven-Hundred-Foot mine.

John Treadwell sold his interest in the Treadwell Gold Mine for $1,500,000, and returned home to California. John Treadwell and his brother, James, started an investment company in New York, and in 1914, filed for bankruptcy, claiming 3 million dollars in debt with no assets. John Treadwell died on December 6, 1927 at the age of eighty-five. He is buried in New York.

On April 22, 1917, the mines were flooded by salt water, as they had mined below sea level. The Gastineau Channel, which is part of the inside passage, broke through and flooded the mines. The superintendent and three others went into the mine to see that everybody made it out and to determine the extent of the damage. They were lucky to make it out alive, and they did so only because of a skillful hoist engineer.

No miners were thought to have been killed in the flood, though one man was missing. It was commonly thought that he took advantage of the opportunity to disappear. All the horses and mules were abandoned in the mine, as there was no time to rescue them.

"A skillful hoist engineer." This makes me wonder if it was the complaints of the powder men—Edwin, Billy, and others—about the dangerous hoist engineer dropping the cage on several occasions, once when full of volatile explosives, that prompted management to have better-trained hoist engineers. Could it be possible that Edwin, Billy, and the others were indirectly responsible for the superintendent and the three others surviving the flood at Treadwell on April 22, 1917, due to the well-trained hoist engineer thirteen years after Edwin worked at Treadwell? The above statement was written by Barry Kibler.

John Treadwell seated second from right.
P172 -16a Alaska State Library
DeGroff, Edward creator

Acknowledgments

<u>Mrs. Mary Hall of the Alaskan Centers at Ketchikan</u>, for encouraging me to publish the Treadwell diaries. This book would not exist if not for Mary Hall's suggestion to publish the diaries of my grandfather, Edwin Warren.

<u>The Alaska State Library Digital Archives</u>, for images on the Internet and the diaries enhance each other, making it possible to visualize the Treadwell mine and the daily life at Treadwell in a manner that would be impossible to accurately visualize without them.

<u>Sarah Hurst, editor for the *Miner North,* Anchorage, Alaska</u>, for her wonderful two-page spread on February 26, 2006 on the, diaries entitled "Diaries Vividly Depict Mining History," complete with images of the Treadwell mine complex and the Treadwell Express train. The images were provided by the Alaska State Library as well as a family portrait of Edwin Warren from the Kibler collection.

<u>Ben Stone, curator of British / American History at Stanford,</u> for his efforts and interest in the diaries, providing me with Edwin's class picture as well as of his entire class of 1908 and of the front cover of the 1908 yearbook, the *Quad*. Ben has been very helpful throughout the long process of preparing the manuscript for publishing.

<u>Professor Mike Dunning Ph.D., University of Alaska,</u> for his interest and advice concerning the diaries.

Chapter One:
North to Alaska

Presented By : Barry Kibler

April 20, 1903

STARTED FOR ALASKA ON MY WHEEL

[By bicycle, train, and steamship.—Barry Kibler] Started from Pacific Grove, California, for Seattle, Washington. Rode to San Jose on my wheel.

April 21, 1903

SAN JOSE TO STOCKTON ON MY WHEEL

Rode my wheel, from San Jose to Stockton, Ca. ["Wheel" refers to a vintage bicycle of the time period as advised by the wheelman's club and not a high bike or Penny feather ling as I first thought. The terminology continued long after the big wheel was no longer in common use.]

This was a very pleasant ride through pretty country. The road led up from the Santa Clara valley into the foothills, past the mission San Jose, then into the Livermore Valley, through Pleasanton and Livermore, where I had dinner, then through the hills again and out into the San Joaquin plain. I reached Tracey at 3 PM and started for Stockton, which

Edwin Warren

1903 Columbia bicycle (WHEEL)
Jacques Graber Photo collection
Wheelman's bicycle club

I reached about half past six. The distance covered from San Jose to Stockton was about seventy-five miles and the ride most of the day before, from home to San Jose, was eighty miles.

April 22, 1903

SAN JOSE TO SACRAMENTO ON MY WHEEL

Rode to Sacramento, fifty-two miles, arriving there at half past three. Looked about the Capital City until 11 AM the next day, when I took the train for Portland, Oregon.

I remained about five days in Portland, waiting for my things to come from home. In the public park were seven or eight live bald eagles in a large cage. When my things came, I went to Seattle, Washington. I remained there a little less than a week, going to Cloverdale, B.C.

May 6, 1903

SEATTLE TO CLOVERDALE BY TRAIN

I went from Seattle, to Cloverdale, on a railroad pass for company work. I went to work right away in the camp dining room. I worked from May 9th through June 1st, partly inside and partly outside.

BIRDS OBSERVED NEAR CLOVERDALE, B.C.

Bald eagle, turkey buzzard (duck's hawk), desert sparrow hawk, burrowing owl,(short-eared owl), pileated woodpecker, Harris woodpecker, lt. blue heron, flicker, olive-sided flycatcher, Western flycatcher, crow, raven, Western meadowlark, Sony sparrow, Sambel's sparrow, sora rail, russet-backed thrush, Vigor's wren, Western robin, Chinese pheasant, Oregon junco, Oregon towhee, Anna's hummingbird, blue-fronted jay, bush teal, barn swallow, cliff swallow, Western bluebird, purple finches, and chickadee.

I found a robin's nest with newly hatched young; also, a deserted nest containing two eggs. Found another nest with young the next day in a cavity in a fir tree stub, seven feet from the ground. The nest was composed of moss and hair; incubation began.

June 1, 1903

BIRD WATCHING

I found a chickadee's nest containing fully fledged and nearly full-grown young. I found a robin's nest with two newly-hatched young and one egg, also a deserted nest containing two eggs. Found another nest with young the next day.

I collected a nest and two eggs of Anna's hummingbird. The nest was placed on a drooping cedar branch, about seven feet from the ground, near a wagon road in rather thick woods. The bird was very tame, allowing me to place my hand within a few inches of the nest before she would take flight; incubation slight.

June 11, 1903

CLOVER DALE TO VANCOUVER

Took a set of four eggs of western robin from nest placed about twelve feet up in an alder sapling. The nest [was] placed among small twigs against the main stem of the sapling. It was composed of twigs, roots, string, moss, and mud, and lined with dried grass; incubation very slight. I went from Cloverdale to Vancouver. Found that the steamer *Princess May*, was to sail the next evening.

June 12, 1903

ABOARD THE STEAMER *PRINCESS MAY*

I went onboard the steamer *Princess May* to see if I could work my passage. They told me to return in the evening. As it was raining, I went back to my room and wrote a number of letters. One to the folks, one to Merle, one to Roy Well, one to Earle Mylar, one to Ross Brown, and one to A.E. Trowmane. Went on the boat again about 8 PM and saw the officers, but there was no chance to work. I stayed on board all night and the next morning at nine thirty, we started north. Our steamer was about to the Queen Charlotte Sound by dark. We had a very pleasant day and enjoyed the trip very much. We entered the narrows first about suppertime and the scenery was grand.

June 14, 1903

IN THE NARROWS

We were not able to see much when we first got up, on account of the fog, but it soon lifted and we had a fine clear day. The most of the day we were in the narrows, but we passed through the open water of Milbank Sound about noon and were just coming out into Dixon's Entrance as it got dark. [The *Princess May* was later shipwrecked.]

June 15, 1903

ABOARD THE STEAMER *HUMBOLDT*

When we got up this morning, we were still in narrow water and approaching Ketchikan, which we reached at 6:30 AM. I left the *Princess May* here, as this was the point to which I bought my ticket. After making some inquires in regard to work, and not getting very favorable reports, I decided to proceed to Juneau. The *Humboldt* [was] a rival ship which had kept us close company on most of the voyage. Having arrived, I took passage on her for Juneau.

EDWIN WARREN
Kibler Photo collection

Steamer Princess May
UAA - hmc -0428 - series 6 - f1 - 394
Winter & Pond creator
Alaska State Library

P -226 - 314 Alaska State Library
Mexican Mine, Treadwell 1908
Case and Draper creators

Treadwell Mine 1500 ft. level Ready Bullion.
P- 40 -21 Alaska State Library
Case W.H. creator

Chapter Two:
The Treadwell Gold Mine

June 16, 1903

I AM NOW A TREADWELL MINER

I landed at Douglas city, opposite Juneau about four AM. Had breakfast and then went to the Treadwell mine to see about work. Was told to report at seven o'clock in the evening and go on night shift.

June 24, 1903

SUFFERING FROM THE GAS

Have been working in the mine one week. The gas and smoke have bothered me a good deal, making my head ache. Last night, the boss put me in a different part of the mine and I got along better.

July 1, 1903

CROW-HOPPING RAVENS

I have seen, but very few birds around here as yet. There are a good many ravens and Northwest crows along the waterfront. The ravens have a very comical way of hopping. Doubtless the expression "crow-hopping" was derived from them.

July 4, 1903

BIRD WATCHING

Today, I noticed quite a number of small gulls or terns on the water. They were quite small and those in full plumage had black heads and red or pink feet. They were smaller than Bonaparte's gull.

July 5, 1903

A REMARKABLE MAN

I have just finished reading *The Making of an American* by Jacob A. Riis. It is a well-told story of the life work of a remarkable man. With him, [the] will was to accomplish, though it took years. Once determined on a course, he would persevere through all kinds of difficulties until he saw the hoped-for results. Coming to this country from Denmark when a young man, he saw many trials and hardships before he finally became a reporter in New York. He threw all his energies into reform work and probably had more influence in the improvement of the conditions of the tenements and the schools and parks in the crowded districts than any other one man.

Edwin Warren

July 22, 1903

AUDUBON DONATION

Daily Dispatch, Juneau: An item was in one of the daily papers, giving a list of contributors to the St. Louis Brooders mentions the sum of fifteen thousand dollars donated by the Audubon Society for the passage of its bill.

July 28, 1903

THE FIRST ICEBERGS I'VE SEEN

This evening, there are several pretty good-sized chunks of ice floating in the channel. They are the first "icebergs" I have seen.

July 29, 1903

I FAINTED FROM THE EFFECTS OF THE GAS

The last day or two, there has been a great deal of gas in the mine where I am working. Nearly everyone suffers from it to some extent. I had a very bad headache and some of the others were too sick to work out the full shift. I fainted from the effects of the gas in the mine one day, at the station just before going up on the skip. We were all standing around waiting for the skip.

The smoke and gas were pretty thick and I felt myself getting dizzy. I took a good hold of the ore car against which I was leaning, but almost before I knew it, I lost consciousness and fell flat on my face. The boys picked me up and I gradually came to and was all right as soon as I got on top. I believe that is the only time I have fainted in my life.

July 30, 1903

LETTER FROM MARGARET WARREN

It has been raining all the afternoon. A boat came in early this morning and as I thought I might get a letter, I went down to the post office. Found a nice letter there from Merle. Last night, I got a letter from Margaret; it took the letter twelve days to come here from Honolulu. She had not yet received my letter. [It is unknown who Merle was possibly a lady friend, Margaret was Edwin's sister.]

July 31, 1903

BIRD WATCHING

This evening, I took quite a long walk. I went down through Douglas City, and then along the bluff, past the cemetery to opposite Juneau. It was a beautiful, clear evening. The water below me was a deep green color and as smooth as glass. A few gulls were flying slowly over the water, and once a flock of ducks or scooters rose from before a passing launch. I saw a number of robins and juncos among the undergrowth along the road. There were a few ripe salmon berries along the way, but they had been pretty well picked over. Several other kinds of blueberries were plentiful, but I did not care to experiment as to their value as food.

The days are getting noticeably shorter now, and I suppose before long, winter will be here. I have been thinking some of getting a shotgun and trying to collect a few birds, but I have so little time, and birds are so scarce that I don't believe it will be worthwhile. If I stay here this winter, I will get all ready for a big collecting trip next June to Sitka or Dutch Harbor or some other good locality on the Alaskan coast. It has been my fond dream for years to spend a season collecting in Alaska.

I had hoped to be able to do some collecting this season, but got here too late and had to go right to work. I have not fully decided whether to stay here this winter or go home, but I think I will stay here.

If I do, I will be able to save several hundred dollars towards going to college, as well as having the pleasure of gathering sea birds' eggs next summer. No doubt, the winters will be long and cold and working in the mine very disagreeable at times, though.

But then, others stand it without any special aim or object in view, so I guess I can get though it all right when I think of the "good times coming." But whether I stay or go, I am pretty sure of some good times and advantages wherever I am. When I think of going home, I regret losing my chance at the sea birds, and when I conclude to stay here, I sigh for my old range among the golden eagles' nests of old Monterey and San Benito counties. However, I will undoubtedly have a good many more opportunities to renew my acquaintance with the golden eagles than I will with the birds of Alaska.

July 29, 1903

MEN WAITING FOR DINNER

This noon, some traveling photographers took pictures of the men running down from the mine to dinner, with bioscope (or moving picture) cameras. We all ran with a will, as usual, and the scene of several hundred men in that rush down the hill will no doubt be interesting.

August 1, 1903

FIRST PAYDAY

Today, I had the pleasure of receiving my first pay as a miner. I have worked six weeks, but only got one month's pay as they hold two weeks' pay in the office until you quit. I had to wait a good while in line before I could get my pay. I drew $50.30, which was coming to me, after my store bill, hospital, and library fees were deducted. I went downtown as soon as I had cleaned up a bit and got a money order for $48.00, which I sent home with the request that $10.00 be forwarded to Margaret at once, and the rest used for my insurance, etc.

This is the first money I have sent home since leaving in April. Lots of the boys are spending their money downtown tonight having a "good time," as they think. After getting the P.O. money order, I came up to the library and wrote a letter home. Also, [I wrote] one to Merle then went upstairs for a while to an entertainment that was going on. It was a rather light comedy entitled *The Deacon's Waterloo*. I dropped my watch, breaking the crystal. This evening, I went to the Indian mission. There were not many present, but there were several earnest native Christians; the mission is conducted by the Friends.

August 3, 1903

WROTE TO MARGARET

Wrote to Margaret. [Edwin's sister, a missionary in Hawaii.]

August 4, 1903

SLOVENIAN HOLIDAY

Today was a big day with the Slavs. They had celebration at their church, for the laying of the cornerstone, I believe, though the church was built a year ago. Most of the Slovenians in the mine took a holiday. As Mike, the bulldozer man, was out, I had to attend to his duties. Nearly every other one of them seems to be named Mike. "Mike the Bulldozer" is quite a character. He knows very little English, but endeavors to supply the deficiency by a liberal use of choice English profanity, of which he has good command. If these fellows would do their swearing in their native tongue, it would be less tiresome. I attended the missions again tonight. The workers are very friendly and give me cordial invitations to the meetings. Expected a letter from home tonight, but it did not come. Instead, I got one from Benj Heoag, enclosing prices on ornithological books and periodicals; I would like to get a lot of them. I believe I would spend half my wages for books if I could. The new edition of *Bones Key*, in two volumes, I simply must have. It is not out of the publisher's hand as yet; however, it is no doubt the best all-around work on the birds of North America ever published. I have a copy of the old edition, but it is badly out of date. It was published a good many years ago.

August 5, 1903

THREE KILLED & THREE INJURED

The first thing I heard this morning was that three men had been killed, and as many more badly injured, in the mine on the night shift. The wheel over which the shop cable runs [over the] top of the hoist had broken and the jar had caused the cable to break. The skip loaded with ore dropped from the surface to the bottom of the shaft, killing two men and injuring several others. The third man killed was one of the hoist engineers who was struck by the broken cable. I only knew one of the men—a young Italian. It was his first night's work in the shaft. Today, I have been helping the powder man.

We did not get dinner until four o'clock, but it was well worth waiting for: nice fried eggs and porterhouse steak. It's the first time since I've been here that we had either eggs or steak cooked to my taste. We got through work about half past four, and I took a walk down the track past the Mexican and Ready Bullion mines. I had a regular feast on salmon berries, which I found in abundance. There were also a good many blue berries of some [sort] but as I did not know what they were, I did not sample them.

August 6, 1903

NEAR RIOT AT TREADWELL

This evening, I went down town and got the mail. [I] had a letter from home, [and] also one from Margaret in Honolulu. Both were very cheering. I met an Indian girl on the track who had several buckets of blue berries such as I saw yesterday. After this, I will not be afraid to eat them. There came near to being a general mix-up between the Slavs and white men tonight. [The] fight was on between a big Slav and one of the blacksmiths, and the Slavs were not giving them a fair show. The Americans wanted to separate them and the Slavs began to mix things. Several fights were on and a general riot was in danger when the hose was turned on and cooled things down a bit.

August 6, 1903

NEAR EXPLOSION AT TREADWELL

I am still helping the powder man, and so do not have to change shifts. Today, we were bringing up a load of caps from the magazine and we came near having a collision with the train in the six hundred level. We had five boxes of caps in the truck, and Billy, the powder man, went ahead to have the train stop until we got out. He told the conductor we were coming out, and the conductor said he would tell the engineer and they would not come back until we got through. But when we started in, the conductor forgot all about us and failed to tell the engineer.

When about halfway through the level, the cable began to move and Billy ran ahead. He met the train and yelled to the conductor, who jumped off and gave the signal on the wires with his candle sticks to stop. Billy tried to signal by pressing the wires together, but it did not seem to work. The train did not stop until it was within a couple of feet of the truck. If they had come together there would have almost certainly been an explosion, and if there had, I would not be writing this. It happened so quickly that I hardly had time to get scared before the danger was over.

P87- 2981 Alaska state library
Treadwell ore train
Case & Draper creators

Drusilla Warren,
Edwin's stern Methodist mother
Kibler Photo collection

Margaret Warren, Edwin's sister
A missionary in Hawaii.
She contracted TB while tending the ill.
She died at twenty-seven years of age,
and was buried in Pacific Grove, Ca.
Kibler Photo collection

Los Pinos lighthouse, Pacific Grove, Ca.
Barry Kibler creator

Edwin's father, mother, and sister are buried in the cemetery behind the Los Pinos lighthouse in Pacific Grove, California, at the end of Lighthouse Ave. Edwin Warren SN., Drusilla Warren, and Margaret Warren.

August 10, 1903

A RAINY DAY

It is raining today. Drew Nauseas's *Farthest North* from the library.

August 17, 1903

TWO MEN KILLED; MANY NOW QUITTING

For the last few days, the weather has been delightfully clear; bright days without wind. Billy, the powder man, has gone on a trip back East, and I am holding down his job. I have two young Swedes as helpers now. One of them just started work a couple of days ago and suffers a good deal from the gas. Before he began work, a college student from Seattle was helping me. He is working over on the Juneau side now, helping the survivors. Yesterday afternoon, there were two men killed in one of the 440 stopes by a slab of rock dropping on them. They were running a machine; both were Swedes. Quite a few are quitting now.

August 18, 1903

A WEALTH OF PLEASURE AND INFORMATION

After supper this evening, I saw quite a large flock of gulls on the beach by the boarding house. I sat down close by and watched them for quite a while. There were three or four different species. There were several stages of plumage represented, so I couldn't tell exactly how many species there were. There were a good many small gulls about the size of *Larus philadelphia,* then a size intermediate between them, and the large common gulls which I suppose are the glancous-winged gulls. The small gulls were in beautiful plumage, and I could have secured a fine series if I had had a gun. How I would like to be able to secure some good specimens. I am unable to tell what species the different birds belong to, and so lose the greatest good of my observations. What a wealth of pleasure and information there would be in a good series of these and other Alaskan birds, and they would never be missed from the millions that swarm the coast. I am eagerly looking forward to the time when I shall be able to do some scientific collecting.

August 19, 1903

DROPPED THE CAGE WITH MEN UNDERWATER

There are a couple of steamers at the Treadwell wharf this morning, and a number of visitors have been around the mine. I finished my work about 10:45 this morning, and am sitting out in the fresh air near the primer house, writing. I have nothing more to do before noon but to give my powder report. It is beginning to get a little cloudy and we may have rain soon.

The last letter I had from home told of a Mr. Eddy who, with his family, had rented our cottage. He has made several trips to Alaska and owns property at the mouth of the Copper River. He told the folks that I could get work at Wrangell anytime at wages from seventy five dollars per month and board up.

The fare there from here is about twenty dollars. I have half a notion to go there, but am afraid it will be almost too late in the season. I think it might be a more favorable locality than this, from an ornithological standpoint. Where I would like to go would be Dutch Harbor—if I thought I could get work there.

I think that I can undoubtedly spend the collecting season to better advantage there or near there than most anywhere else. It would be a big help to be there for some time previous to the beginning of the season, in order to get acquainted with the locality. Part of my duties as powder man consists of running the station pump at the shaft where we bring down powder. As we were taking powder in the magazine yesterday, I did not have time to run the pump, and this afternoon, the water was standing in the drift several inches above the top of the shaft. I soon got the pump started, and before long, the water was down low enough to allow us to get on the cage. Sometime before I came here, the engineer dropped the cage with two or three men down thirty or forty feet under water. He pulled them up again, however, before they were much damaged.

August 20, 1903

CHAPLAIN CLEMMENS

It is raining lightly this morning. Last night when I went home, I found quite a bunch of mail on the table, which Elmer had brought up from town. There was a letter from Murray, from Colfax, and a package of data which he had printed for me. There was a fine long letter from the folks, enclosing one from a collector in the East who wanted to exchange for some eagle eggs. He sent quite a list of eggs, by their A.O.U. numbers, but not names.

As I have no catalogue with me, I cannot tell just what he has to offer. However, I do not want to trade any of my eagle eggs at present. If I ever have any more than I want, I will only trade them for especially desirable sets. The folks said in their letter that Chaplain Clemmens had learned to cut up bird skins.

When I first got acquainted with him, he leaned quite strongly toward the Audubon Society way of thinking—and not the way of good old Audubon, to whom the shotgun was a constant and beloved companion; but the way [of] his more timid namesakes, who hunted birds with a campstool and a pair of opera glasses.

I remember a visit the chaplain and I made to Mr. George Brenninger, when that gentleman was collecting birds at Pacific Grove. We found Mr. Brenninger in his work room at the laboratory, surrounded by a goodly number of choice bird skins which he had been putting up. We had a very pleasant visit, but afterwards, the chaplain told me he did not approve of the work Mr. Brenninger was doing, that is, killing birds for specimens. And now he has learned to put up bird skins. But by the interest he took in my collection, both of birds and eggs, I knew he was not cut out to be a strict Audubon. I would not be surprised at any time to hear that he had begun a collection of eggs.

Were I at home now, I am sure he would prove both interested and an interesting companion on various collecting trips. Today, I am putting in spare time in looking up the different places west of here where I might be able to get work for the winter. In the summer, there is work to be had almost anywhere, but in the winter, most of the smaller mines shut down, and of course, fisheries only run in the summer. I think Kodiak Island would be a good place to go, but I am not sure about work.

It is not only a good locality itself, but it would be a good starting point for my main trip next June. Sometime ago, I wrote home for some of my skinning tools and reloading outfit. They came last night and I don't know when I will have a chance to use them. Soon, I hope. Today, I came across a report on the geology and gold mines of southeastern Alaska; it contains a number of fine illustrations and a good deal of valuable information. It has a good deal in it about the Treadwell Mines; I think I will write to the Geological Survey at Washington for a copy of this and other reports.

August 21, 1903

RAVENS AND CROWS ON LITTLE JUNEAU ISLAND

We are having alternate periods of sunshine and clouds today. As I write, I can see the sun shining on the buildings over in Juneau, which on this side [of] the landscape is under shadow. Now the sun comes out again, and its cheering warmth soon makes itself felt clear to your backbone. I have not seen any ravens or crows lately; they were very numerous through the early part of the summer, and their croaking's were to be heard on all sides. The pair of bald eagles which I noticed at first has also disappeared. One of the first things I saw when I landed on this island was a bald eagle perched in a dead tree on the little Juneau Island in the channel.

August 22, 1903

ONE COULD SEE WONDERFUL THINGS

It was another pleasant day; I take especial note of all the fine days we get now as we can't expect to get many more of them. This morning, I wrote to Dr. C. Hart [in] Merrian, Washington, in regard to government reports of Alaskan ornithology. I don't know whether there have been any such reports published or not. Last night, I went to Christian Endeavors at the Friends' church. Stopped at the post office on the way and got a letter from Emma. When I came home, it was a beautiful, clear night; no moonlight, but still not dark. The mountains across the channel cast their dark shadows into the still water, and over their tops to the northward was a soft, mellow light. It seems as if one could see wonderful things from those summits on a night like this.

August 23, 1903

WORKING ON SUNDAYS

This is a beautiful, warm Sunday; I wish I did not have to work on Sundays, without the Sabbath for rest and mental and spiritual improvement. The week goes by in a rather monotonous way, week in and week out, nothing but work. No day to call your own in which you can rise above your daily cares. Change day and I am waiting for the second dinner. I am sitting on the back steps of the Bear's Nest boarding house as I write. The *City of Topeka* is at the Treadwell wharf. Flying around or resting idly in the water are numerous gulls of several different species. A few chunks of ice are floating in the channel. The water is still and blue, except where the passage is narrow and the mountains rise close to the water. There it is deep green reflected from the verdure on the mountain sides; the scene is one of peace and beauty. Today, I have been reading a number of articles in the *Christian Endeavor World*, which a lady gave me last Friday night.

August 24, 1903

WORKING WITH A DANGEROUS MAN

This is as beautiful a day as I ever saw anywhere, I believe. I am basking in the sunshine near the primer house. Mr. Watson, the primer man, says that this is one of the finest summers he has seen in Alaska. I now have to come out of the mine quite a number of times during the forenoon after primers, and I enjoy the fresh air and sunshine very much. It makes the day go by much more pleasantly than when you have to stay underground all the time. I generally finish my work about eleven o'clock in the forenoon and five in the afternoon.

I have to hang up the checks in the office just before six o'clock. The engineer—who has been running the seven hundred hoist where we lower our powder—has lost his job. He let the cage load of powder drop seven or eight feet and strike a bulkhead below the six hundred level. That was just before Billy quit, and he reported it to the assistant foreman.

Then, a couple of days ago, he dropped the cage in the same way and a lot of slack cable with it. As we did not care to take any chances with an incompetent man, [we] reported it to the foreman and told him we did not care to lower powder to that engineer. So he took him away and was going to put him to dumping cars, but he quit. The look he gave me at the table the next morning was anything but pleasant. There were others who had worked in that shaft who were afraid to work there with him as he was not a competent man; some said he had never run an engine before.

In looking over the first part of my diary, I find that I have made no mention of the nest I found near Cloverdale which I took to be a duck hawk's. As I was much interested in it and spent considerable spare time in watching it, I will give a brief account of it here.

A few days after I went to work at the railroad camp near Cloverdale, I was riding on the work train, taking the men's dinner out to where they were at work. As usual, I was on the lookout for nests, and presently, I spied one built right on top of a tall dead tree which stood a half mile or so back on the hillside. I saw a bird of some kind fly to the nest, so determined to find out what kind it was, although from the size and height of the tree, I judged it to be well near-to -impossible to climb. A couple of days later, I had an hour or two to spare, so went up to the place.

As I approached, I could see one of the old birds perched in a nearby tree. I could tell it was a hawk of some kind, but I did not recognize the species. When I got quite close, it began to squeal or cackle, very much as the prairie falcon does. At the same time, its mate flew from the nest. I had never seen a duck hawk, but I had heard them described, and from the cackling noise they made, I judged them to belong to the species. I have always been very anxious to secure some of their eggs, and so was delighted at my discovery. I now began to size up the tree, and see if there was not some way to climb it.

It was an enormous dead fir with the top broken off. [It] was almost entirely devoid of limbs. Leaning against it was another tree, only slightly smaller, which had been chopped nearly through, and in falling, had lodged against it, some thirty or forty feet from the top. But either tree was by far to big to grasp in climbing, so the only way I could see to get up was to drive in spikes to stand on and hold on to, driving them in above me as far as I could reach. Then standing on them and driving in others still higher up, in another day or so. I again had a little spare time, so I armed myself with hatchet and what few spikes I had.

They numbered only about eight or nine, but I was determined to get up as far as I could with them, and then, if need be, come down and procure more spikes and finish the job another day. The first thing I did was to cut a small sapling which grew near the base of the leaning tree, in such a manner that it leaned over against the trunks of the ladder. I could easily climb the sapling and this gave me a start of some thirty feet.

There I drove in a spike to stand on, and another higher up to hold on to, and still another as far above my head as I could reach. Then stepping up one spike, I would drive in another above me. In trying to make my spikes go as far as possible, I got them almost too far apart. When I had used them all, and was trying to get a grip of the tree to pull myself up higher, I felt myself slipping. When I tried to get hold of a spike, I could not find one.

I kept slipping, and was just on the point of sliding off the tree when my coat sleeve caught on a spike and held me. I lost no time in gaining a secure hold and made my way to the ground as soon as I could. I had found out that the tree was scaleable, however provided I had plenty of spikes. I went into Cloverdale, but could not get any. The nearest place I could get them was New Westminster. I could not get a day off, so quit my job knowing I could get it back or another as good. The next day, I went to Westminster on the train, having secured a hospital pass from the timekeeper. I went to a hardware store and bought sixty-five large spikes for twenty-five cents.

As there was no return train until the next day, I had to walk back. I did not get home until nearly ten o'clock PM, having gotten on a wrong road. It was very dark and raining heavily before I reached camp. The next day, I took spikes and hatchet and again went to the tree. The birds were both around. I now used as many spikes as necessary to make climbing safe. Without a great deal of trouble, but with great caution, I made my way gradually into the tree. When nearly to the top, I was able to get along with a few spikes as there were some broken-off limbs.

I could not get above the rim of the nest to look in, but by holding my pocket mirror above it, I could see that the nest contained no eggs.

This was quite a disappointment, but still, I thought they would lay soon and I could get them later. I watched them a great deal after that; the birds were always near the nest, perched in their tall trees. I kept track of them for nearly a month, and finally climbed to the nest the day before I left for Vancouver, but it was as empty as before.

The nest was between one hundred and twenty five and one hundred and fifty feet from the ground. Before leaving, I came to the conclusion that I was mistaken in their identity, and that they were ospreys, or fish hawks instead of duck hawks.

This was one of the hardest climbs I have ever taken, and had I secured a set of duck hawks, I would have felt amply repaid. I would not have climbed the tree in the first place for a set of osprey eggs, but after getting in the spikes, I would have considered a set of them as being some compensation for my trouble. But we cannot expect success every time. I learned a good many interesting points from my observation of the birds, so the time spent was not entirely without reward. There was a huge nest of the bald eagle in the top of a large tree not far from the osprey's nest. I do not think it was occupied, though I sometimes saw eagles in the vicinity. One day, one of the eagles flew near the osprey's nest, and both of the owners immediately set off in pursuit, squealing and cackling. I was sorry to lose my hatchet in the fallen timber near the eagle's nest and I had no chance of finding it, as I could not retrace my steps, owing to the thick tangle of fallen trees, undergrowth, and decaying logs. It was the thickest and most difficult place to navigate in I have struck yet.

Edwin Warren

August 25, 1903

RAIN SOON

It is quite dark and cloudy today with some wind from the south. We will probably have rain before long.

August 26, 1903

ELEMENTS OF GEOLOGY

Last night, I received a short letter from Margaret. After I returned from town, I finished reading the first volume of *Mansen's Farthest North*.

There is a good deal in it to interest and instruct, but it is necessarily monotonous in some places, as any record of living ice-bound on a small ship for months at a time must be. As soon as I finish the second volume, I intend to take up LeLeontis's *Elements of Geology*, and make as thorough a study of the subject as time will allow. It is a standard work, and right up to date. I may find parts of it rather difficult to grasp, but I think I can learn a good deal from it. I am more impressed than ever with the necessity of making use of all the time possible in study. I am awed when I think of the vast fields of science.

[There are] so many branches of scientific research in which I am interested and about which I know so little. A lifetime spent in solving the mysteries of a single science is all too short to fathom its depths. How then can I hope to gain access to them all? I believe the best plan is to try and learn the elements, that is, the most important parts of those studies which interest me, and then make a specialty of one or two others, trying to become well-versed in them. So many of the sciences are so closely related that the pursuit of one leads you on and on from one field of knowledge to another. But many lines of study must be ignored entirely, in order to progress with others.

August 27, 1903

FOGGY DAYS

It has been quite foggy and cloudy for the past two or three days with occasional showers.

August 28, 1903

A SCENE OF LIFE AND BEAUTY

A nice, bright day again. The powder boat, the *Al-Ki,* came in this morning. My work will be some less now as we have been out of priming powder for some time and have had to use the full-size No. 1 powder, which is just twice as heavy as the priming powder. I saw two or three ravens yesterday. I don't know whether any of them remain here through the winter or not. I have been down to the post office for the last three nights, but have not received any letters. Last night, the *Dirigo* came in the night before the *Humboldt*, and the day before that, the *City of Topeka*.

I am liable to quit going to the post office for a while so as to be sure of something when I do go. Just now, I am sitting outside by the edge of the channel, waiting for another trainload of powder to put into the magazine. A large flock of pretty white gulls [is] circling around in front of me, or swimming lightly on the quiet water; they make a scene full of life and beauty. I have got lots of help today. Besides my two regular helpers, I have got four husky Slovenians to rustle in powder.

This is more than can work to advantage, as we get in each other's way, so we let the Slavs do most of the work, and we see that they do it right.

Edwin Warren

August 29, 1903

LAND BIRDS OF MONTEREY

We did not finish with the powder until about eight o'clock last night, but we got a good supper when we did get through. Just my regular helpers and I worked overtime When we went in to supper, we found on each of our plates three nicely fried eggs and some fried potatoes. Then there was a platter of porterhouse steaks, properly cooked—not stewed, as usual. We did full justice to it, and did not leave any for the cooks to warm over. Then there was pie, cookies, etc.

The *Dolphin* came in this morning, and as I knew she must bring some mail for me, I hurried up my dinner and went down to the post office at noon. I was well pleased at getting letters from Merle, Emerson, Grinnell, and the folks. It will keep me busy writing letters for a while now.

Grinnell is preparing a paper [entitled] "Land Birds of Monterey and Vicinity." He wishes me to contribute some notes on migration and nesting dates. I wrote home last night for my notebooks, and will give him what help I may be able.

September 2, 1903

PAYDAY

Another gray day has come and gone. Last night, I drew fifty dollars and fifteen cents, just fifteen cents less than last month. Went down to the post office and got money orders for forty-five dollars of which, I sent forty dollars home to pay my insurance. I sent two dollars to Grinnell for my club dues, and three dollars to Emerson for four volumes of the *Ideologist*. This morning, one of my helpers failed to appear. He probably got too much tangle foot last night.[He got lucky]

September 3, 1903

THE NOTORIOUS TOUGH, RED NELSON

Last night, I attended an auction sale downtown. Bought a shaving set for one dollar, consisting of a razor, strap, brush, six cakes of soap, and five assorted combs. No doubt, the razor will prove to be the kind that is made to sell, but not to shave with. Coming along the trestle towards home, I met one of the boys who said there was a man lying on the tracks just ahead. It proved to be Red Nelson, a notorious tough who had formerly worked in the mine. He was dead drunk. How he had ever been able to keep his footing on that narrow trestle and get as far as he did without falling off is a mystery to me. Some men came with a wheelbarrow and we put him in it and got him to his room.

September 4, 1903

SUNNY DAYS

The fine weather still continues—no rain, no wind, no cold—just bright, clear, sunshiny days.

September 6, 1903

THE TREADWELL GHOST

Sunday evening, I did not go to church tonight, as it is raining. The rain began last night. The large mill has been shut down for several days because of the shortage of water, so I guess the company is glad of the rain, anyhow. The latest sensation is furnished by Dick Thompson and others claiming to have seen a ghost in the mine. It appeared in hip-boots and slicker, according to the account, and finally disappeared through a raise, climbing up hand over hand on an invisible rope. I hope it doesn't show itself to me.

September 13, 1903

THE CHRISTIAN ENDEAVORS

The weather for the past week has been mostly clear and pleasant. It is raining again this morning, however. Last night, I wrote letters until eleven o'clock as I wanted to get them off on the *Cottage City*. Yesterday, I began on LeCeonte's *Elements of Geology*. I am going to make a synopsis or summary of it as I go. It now appears that the ghost which appeared to Dick was especially prepared for the occasion by some of the boys, and let down by a string into the pit where he was working. Dick was fired for circulating his ghost yarn, as the bosses were afraid it would cause some of the men to quit.

Several students from the University of Wash. have been working here this summer. I have had one of them, Herbert Jebroth, on the powder gang for some time. They are going back to Seattle this week, as school is to commence soon. I went to Christian Endeavors Friday night; Mr. Jackson was not there.

He was moving the school house over to the mainland, below Sheep Creek. He had it loaded on a barge and was floating it down with the tide. The missionaries have a claim of about four miles [of] frontage there, and they are going to put up the schoolhouse in order to hold it. I believe they are looking toward having an Indian settlement there in the future.

If the Indians could be kept away from the white people, it would be a great deal easier to civilize and Christianize them. Where there is one white missionary working to uplift the natives, there are a hundred whites doing all they can to degrade them. I saw a great blue heron flying overhead day before yesterday. It was the first one I had seen.

September 14, 1903

BALD EAGLES SPOTTED TODAY

This morning, I saw three bald eagles flying above the channel, and this afternoon, there was a bunch of six of them circling the top of the ridge above the Treadwell. It has been damp weather for several days now. After supper, it was raining steadily, but when I stepped out, about eight o'clock, it was clear and the stars were shining.

It is getting dark early now; winter is close at hand. Last night, I received two publications from the geological survey, USGS Bulletins #19 and #21. One tells of the natural history of the Queen Charlotte Islands and the Iwok's Inlet region. The other is an account of a trip up the Yukon River valley by W.H. Osgood and Dr. Louis B. Bishop. Osgood was one of the charter members of the Copper Club. Dr. Bishop looked over my birds and eggs while in Pacific Grove this summer, and spoke quite highly of my work.

September 19, 1903

SAN FRANCISCO FIRE DEPARTMENT

Jack Loftis, one of my powder gang, quit this morning. He got word last night that he had been appointed to a place in the San Francisco Fire Department. I will now have the doubtful pleasure of breaking in a couple of new helpers. [Jack Loftis was undoubtedly a fireman during the 1906 San Francisco fire and earthquake, which also did extensive damage to Stanford University while Edwin was attending in the years of 1904 -1908.]

Edwin Warren

September 20, 1903

THE NATIVE MISSION

This has been a nice, clear day. It seemed fine to see the sun shining bright and warm after a good deal of fog and rain. At six PM tonight, the Treadwell time was set ahead forty minutes on account of the short days. We will now go to work at six twenty AM and quit at five twenty PM; correct time.

Last night, I wrote the folks that I might start for home about the first week in November. This is according to a recent plan of mine to go home for the winter, and then to return to Alaska early in the spring, say about the first of April. I think it would be worthwhile to spend some time at home, as I may be away a good deal in the future. Tonight I went to the Mission for the natives "Presbyterian"; there was quite a good attendance, the meeting was led by the regular pastor, Mr. Jones; a well-educated native translated for him.

September 23, 1903

THE BEAR'S NEST BOARDING HOUSE IS COLD

Yesterday morning and the day before, we had quite a frost. The air was sharp enough to be invigorating and I enjoyed it very much. Last night, the wind blew pretty hard. There is about half a pane of glass out of my window, and the wind blew in. I had to get up and stuff an old pair of pants into the aperture. It had been raining quite hard most all day, and was still at it.

I got my oil pants out of the place where I had hid them over the jump in the mine; I had found that they had gotten quite mildewed. I had a letter from Grinnell day before yesterday in regards to my notes on Monterey birds, so I am putting in spare moments jotting down a few notes from memory, that is, general notes. My notebooks have not arrived yet from home, so, of course, I can't give dates.

September 26, 1903

THE TREADWELL BAND

Tonight, there was a free concert at the YMCA. The Treadwell Band, a recent organization, made its first public appearance. Its part of the program was very mild, as might be expected. Some very good things were rendered in the way of vocal music. Yesterday, I was talking to a man who works in the foundry. He and a companion shot sixty-four ptarmigan over on the Sheep Creek Mountain.

September 30, 1903

SNOWFALL

The last few days there has been quite a snowfall on the surrounding mountains. The air is beginning to get chilly in the evenings. Went to the library this evening and wrote a letter to Murray. As I came home, about half past nine, the moon—about half full—was just to be seen over the tops of the mountains.

October 3, 1903

ANOTHER MAN KILLED TODAY

There was a man killed today in the mine by rocks dropping; two machine men had a narrow escape, as the rock just grazed them. It has been bright and clear today.

October 6, 1903

TREADWELL POST OFFICE

Rather damp today. The *Cottage City* came in this morning at noon. I went down to the Douglas post office, but did not get anything. Came back and got a letter from Merle at the Treadwell post office. This evening, I answered Merle's last two letters, then came home and wrote about nine pages of bird notes, or rather compiled them from my notebooks and memory. It brings back old times to look over my notebooks for the last few years. The records there bring to mind some of the happiest days of my life.

October 14, 1903

BAD WEATHER, GOOD FOOD

It has been raining quite steadily for the last two or three days. For supper tonight, we had venison stew; it was very good.

October 15, 1903

WINTER IS HERE

This morning, when Tom came in from work, he said, "It's a beautiful morning, Ed." I asked him if it was raining and he said no. Then I asked him if it was clear, and he said, "No, it's not exactly clear." When I got up and looked out the window, I saw that everything was white with snow. It was still coming down, and it continued to fall till the middle of the forenoon. How queer it seems to see all the trees and bushes all loaded down with snow. Billy Arthur, the powder man, returned a few days ago, and is going to work tomorrow; I suppose I will be kept on the job as a helper.

October 16, 1903

STILL SNOWING

Several inches of snow fell last night and this forenoon. This afternoon, it has been raining and it is getting pretty sloppy underfoot.

October 23, 1903

WATER IN THE MINE

This evening, I came down to Douglas, and am writing in the barber shop until it is time to go to Christian Endeavors church. I got two letters that have been here since the fourteenth. Since the bad weather has set in, I get my mail at Treadwell: one was from Margaret, the other from Jonathan Dwight of New York. Yesterday and the day before, it rained very hard, and the water came up a good deal in the mine. On the two hundred twenty, level, it was about three feet deep and was confined by bulkheads.

October 30, 1903

WHALES SPOUTING

There have been a number of whales spouting in the channel the last two or three days. It is raining most every day now.

November 7, 1903

CAGE TENDER

This afternoon, I was given the job of cage tender in the Treadwell. The pay is twenty-five cents more than what I have been getting.

Edwin Warren

Last night, we got paid, I sent ten dollars home today. At present, I am reading Drummond's *Ascent of Man*. I have finished this new evangelism. Last night, I mailed my notes to Grinnell; there were about sixty pages of them. I have been getting some very nice specimens of ore lately—several good species—I found near an old prospect tunnel above the seven hundred mine.

Chapter Three:
Homeward Bound To Pacific Grove, CA.

November 14, 1903

FAREWELL TO TREADWELL

A few days ago, I got a letter from home saying that I was needed there, and to come as soon as possible, so yesterday, I quit at the mine and drew my time. I received $127.65. I would have had a little more, but have just been buying a slicker and pair of rubber shoes, with the expectation of staying here through the winter. At noon, I was told that the steamer *Valencia* was across at Juneau, and that she would sail from Treadwell in the evening, so I went home before three o'clock and got everything, including my bedding, packed up. Brown and I carried them up to the store at suppertime. The wind was very high and the *Valencia* did not put in an appearance during the evening. I stayed at the YMCA until nearly eleven o'clock, then took my blankets and went back to the room and went to bed.

Edwin Warren

November 15, 1903

BEAR'S NEST BOARDING HOUSE

 This morning, I got up later than usual and found that the boat had come up to the Treadwell wharf during the night. I went down to Douglas and got my breakfast, then took the ferry and crossed to Juneau, [where I] spent some time looking around the town. Then attended the service at the native church; there were about thirty-five adult Indians present besides children. I doubt that any of the churches of the white people could show as large a number. I had dinner in a restaurant, and then went to the wharf, but the one PM boat had just gone. The ferry time is faster than the standard. Will now have to wait till three o'clock, which I regret, as I hear that the *Valencia* may pull out any time. This morning at the Treadwell, they said she would be there from one to two days loading sulfurites. It has been very cold the last week or so, everything is freezing up and the wind blows so hard you can hardly make your way against it.

 The cold would not be so bad if it were not for the wind. It goes right through the rooms upstairs in the Bear's Nest boarding house, where I have been staying. The windows are not airtight by a good deal, and it was hard to keep warm in bed even.

November 16, 1903

NATIVE VILLAGE OF PETERSBURG

 We got off last night about midnight. The steerage is pretty well crowded. All the bunks are full and mattress are scattered all over the deck. On the table, there is a big stack of mattresses in one corner, and it is on top of that that I roll up in my blankets. There are three others on the same pile, so we don't have much room to kick. It is very cold on board this boat.

This morning as we neared Petersburg, numerous sea birds were seen; there were scoters, murres, murrelets, ducks, cormorants, and pigeon guillemots. It was quite interesting to listen to the remarks of some of the passengers in regard to the birds. Everything is ducks.

A large flock of mures rose from the water and flew past. These were pronounced "butterballs." A short time later, another flock went hurrying by, uttering their weird cries. I was standing beside another group of passengers this time, and they concluded that the birds were teal, and that the noise they made was caused by their wings.

I saw a couple of great blue herons in trees near Petersburg. A few loons were seen. There was a bald eagle's nest nearby, which had a pile of white snow on top instead of the white head of the eagle. At Tonka, in the Wrangell Narrows, the ground was covered with new snow; no snow had fallen at Treadwell for over a week. There is very little wind here today, and some people who came on board at Tonka said that there had been no wind to speak of, quite different from around Douglas Island. We reached Wrangell about four o'clock, and most of us went ashore and took in the sights. There are several huge totem poles around the Indian houses. In port at Kasaan, [we] left about five PM and called at Kasaan on the Prince of Wales Island. About midnight, a young fellow came on board at Wrangle, and hid under the pile of mattresses in the steerage. He was discharged from a boat up here, and is trying to get back to civilization.

November 17, 1903

PORT OF KETCHIKAN

[When] I woke this morning, we were at Ketchikan, I got a bunk this morning that someone had given up. We are now crossing the Dixon's entrance. The crew has just been lashing the loose boxes to the deck, so I suppose we may expect some rough weather. I got rather seasick when we were in the open water.

November 18, 1903

QUEEN CHARLOTTE SOUND

I did not get up to breakfast today, nor to dinner. We got into Queen Charlotte Sound early in the morning, and I felt some what sickish, so I kept to my bunk. Early in the afternoon, I had to get up and raise Jonah, after which I returned to bed. Got into smoother water soon afterwards and felt better.

November 19, 1903

PORT OF SEATTLE

We came through Seymour Narrows during the night, and this morning, were in the Gulf of Georgia. Some fine scenery today; it seems quite different from Alaska. As we are behind time, we did not call at Victoria, but are going right through to Seattle. We passed near Port Townsend just after dinner. It has a nice location. We could see the big guns on the fortifications near by. Surf and white winged scoters are quite plentiful; also occasional cormorants and ducks. Numbers of gulls have been following in the steamer's wake. All through the trip, they are getting bolder all the time. This morning, several of them alit on the upper part of the boat. Reached Seattle about half past three in the afternoon. It was raining, but did not continue very long. I secured a room in the house where I stopped in the spring. Went and got my wheel out of storage.

The man said he thought I was never coming back. The *Queen* is due to sail tomorrow morning to San Francisco and I have a second-class ticket, for which I paid seventy dollars. I would have saved a couple of dollars by getting a through ticket from Douglas, but I did not want to do that, not knowing, but what I might have to wait too long for a boat of the same line.

November 20, 1903

ABOARD THE *QUEEN*

I came down to the wharf this morning about half past eight, and found a big crowd getting their baggage checked. I checked my wheel and then went uptown again as the boat was not to sail till noon. Bought a few apples to take with me. The accommodations are much better on this boat than on the *Valencia*. Here there is a decent dining room and the grub is not thrown at you. The boat is pretty well crowded. There are a couple of my Treadwell friends on board, who left there a few weeks ago.

November 22, 1903

PORT OF VICTORIA

We reached the dock at Victoria about six o'clock, and went up town on the streetcar. Looked around for about an hour; of course, it was too dark to see much of the place, except the business streets. We left about half past eight. When I awoke in the morning, I was soon aware that we were in the open ocean. I felt pretty sick and stayed in my bunk all day, without eating a mouthful. The majority of the passengers were in the same fix, and the cooks and waiters had an easy day. Today, I feel pretty well, though I was weak and dizzy when I first got up. Some of them are still in bed. We haven't had any rough weather, but the boat rolls a great deal. The gulls we see now are much darker on the back than those you see farther north, though a few of the light-backed ones are still to be see. We are getting past the range of the glaucous-winged gull, and into the territory of the Western gull.

Edwin Warren

November 23, 1903

PORT OF SAN FRANCISCO

We reached San Francisco about eleven o'clock, spent the afternoon at Golden Gate Park.

November 24, 1903

SAN FRANCISCO ACADEMY OF SCIENCE

I missed the afternoon train, so am taking the night train. It is 5:45, and the train starts at 6:00 PM. Will get home a little before midnight. I suppose the folks will be astonished to see me at that time of night. Today, I bought a Remington shotgun. Of course, I could have got a cheaper gun, but I wanted something I could depend on.

I spent some time in the Academy of Science today, but did not get a chance to speak to Professor Loomis. I did see the collection of bird skins; the majority of them are very poorly put up. It is quite disgusting to me to see birds on exhibition which are only fit for scarecrows. San Francisco, the birds in the park museum are a better lot than in the academy.

There is a mounted condor in the other place, and two or three in the park. There is also a fine specimen in the aviary, as well as three golden eagles. The eagles were quite noisy, and could be heard screaming for quite a distance.

Margaret's address: 471 Hotel Street, Honolulu, Hawaii c/o Daniel Mission

Dr. Jonathan Dwight 2 E. 34th Street, New York.

[Margaret is Edwin's Sister.]

May 5, 1903

WHEEL STORAGE

Placed bicycle in storage with C.L. Chandler 918 - 920 Third Avenue Seattle, Washington. Rate fifty cents per month or thirty five cents if left more than two months.

END OF FIRST TRIP (1903)

Chapter Four:
Return to Alaska

Start of second trip (1904)

March 30, 1904

ABOARD THE *PUEBLO*

This morning, I left Pacific Grove for Alaska. Mama and Merle walked halfway to the depot with me, and gave me a good sendoff. I rode as far as San Jose with Orrie Hager, who was just starting out for Yosemite. The day was very pleasant, and the fields and the hills a beautiful green. Flaming bunches of California poppies were growing among the grass, adding beauty to the scene. I found James Spencer waiting for me at the depot in San Francisco. After dinner, I went to Clark Wise's music store and had a chat with Leon Francis while James was at the doctor's office. Then we went to a studio and had our likeness taken.

We then went to the Southern Pacific depot and got my luggage. We toted this down to the docks, and I prepared to take my departure. But when I made inquiry at the office of the Dollar Steamship Company, I was told that the *Centennial* would not leave till late tomorrow night.

She was not even in port and still today's paper had her scheduled to sail at 5 PM today. Well, from what I hear about her, I am glad she is behind time. She used to be an old Russian troop ship or something of the kind, and was bought by our government for a transport, but as she was unsatisfactory, she was resold. The *City of Pueblo,* which is a pretty good boat, is due to sail tomorrow at 11 AM, so I expect to go on her. I am writing this in the Francis home in Oakland. Leon wanted me to stay all night, and go across the bay in the morning.

March 31, 1904

SEASICK

Noon: Just outside the golden gate on [the] *Pueblo.* We got off just a little after eleven. The swells of the Pacific are giving us quite a motion, and already, I feel sickish. I have not the slightest desire to go down to dinner, which is now ready below. In fact, I would rather not think of eating as the thoughts of it make me sad. There is quite a crowd on board, including a young married couple, who were showered with rice as they went up the gangplank.

April 1, 1904

BEAUTIFUL WHITE GULLS & ALBATROSSES

I am actually disgusted with myself. We are having fine weather and as good a passage as you could wish, but here I have been seasick nearly all the time. Not deathly sick, but too sick to eat. I have missed four meals straight already. The only thing I have eaten since coming on the boat was one small apple, and that has long since been cast into the sea.

Sea gulls in flight
Barry Kibler creator

I am setting on the fore deck writing, in order to get the fresh air; hundreds of beautiful white gulls are flying about the ship.

They are of two species at least, the Western gull, which is dark blue across the back and wings, and the glaucous-winged gull, which is a light pearly blue on the back. The heads, tails, and under parts of both species are a spotless white. This morning, I saw four albatrosses following in our wake. These are the first I have ever seen, although I have always been on the lookout for them when on the ocean.

April 2, 1904

PORT OF VICTORIA

2:30 PM: We are entering the Straits of Juan de Fuca, and are getting into smoother water. I have kept to my bunk nearly all day. I got up to breakfast, and eat a small dish of mush, which I at once disposed of as food for the fishes. I am feeling better now, and intend to get a good meal on the king's soil this evening in Victoria. We are quite close to the Washington side, which presents a typical scene of heavily forested hills, which rise one above the other as far as you can see. Here and there is to be seen a small group of houses. On the Victoria side, the mountains are higher and more rugged, with patches of snow on their sides. One, Sugarloaf Peak, which we are just passing, is entirely covered with snow. It looks very pretty as the sun shines upon it, making it gleam and sparkle above the dark green hills.

5:00 PM: Well, I have just had a meal, the first on the trip. We got a fairly good supper. There is snow on both sides of us now and it is slightly chilly.

We have several Japanese on board. I heard some of the fellows telling that one of them felt his dinner coming up and not having time to get to the side of the ship, took off his hat and used it for a wash basin, throwing it over board with its load as soon as he reached the rail.

10:30 PM: Have been taking in Victoria for the last three or four hours. We got in just about sundown, so had a chance to see a little before dark. I think it is a very pretty place both in location and construction. I met a young fellow on the street who came to Treadwell shortly before I left. He worked with me half a day, but got scared to work underground and then got a job in the blacksmith shop. He told me tonight that he did not stay long. He has a brother who is running a hoist at Treadwell. He said that he had a letter from him a day or two ago saying that everything was froze up tight, and not many men [were] working. That is rather discouraging news, on top of the information that the YMCA building has been burned.

It seemed almost like a bit of England to walk the streets of Victoria. So many English faces, then lots of Tommy Atkins with their flashy red coats and little round caps on the sides of their heads. They carry themselves as proud as you please, like a lot of game cocks.

Edwin Warren

April 3, 1904

PORT OF SEATTLE

We landed at Seattle about half past six this morning. I got a room right away on First Street near the docks, and then got some breakfast. Found that the barber shops close all day Sunday so got my luggage from the dock and got out my razor and shaved myself. I attended the Easter services at the Methodist church. After dinner, took the car out to 1302 Valley St. and called on Helen and Mary Spencer in the afternoon. Mary took me out to Lake Washington and through Lushi, Madison, and Madrona parks. The lake was beautiful, and the scenery in the parks very pleasing as they are in the natural state. I went to church again in the evening and heard a good musical program.

April 4, 1904

SEATTLE

We are still on board in Seattle. The whistle blew a short time ago and I suppose we will soon be off. The boat is crowded and there are not nearly enough bunks for the second-class passengers. This boat has the reputation of being a pretty good boat, and I guess it is all right for cabin passengers, but the second-class accommodations are about the worst I have seen yet. I am holding down a seat in the main salon and intend to keep it until they give me a berth of some kind.

I had my curtain down in my room last night, and as I was tired and the room so dark, I did not wake until nearly noon. After finishing a letter at the public library, I took the car and rode about seven miles out into the suburbs to my cousin Mary's school at Green Lake.

We took the car to Woodland Park and took a rather lengthy look through it, but as it started to rain, we hurried back to the car line and started toward the city. The shower soon passed over and so we transferred over to the Capitol Hill line and took in Volunteer Park. This is about the highest part of the city, and we could get a good view of the place and its surroundings.

Lake Washington lay on one side, with its deep blue water and background of dark forest. On the other side, we could catch glimpses of Puget Sound, on whose placid waters the sun was casting brilliant patches of light. After enjoying the scene for some time, we returned to Mary's home and enjoyed an excellent supper, which had been prepared by Mrs. Hills, the girl's congenial housekeeper.

We spent an hour visiting in their cozy setting room and then Mary hunted up a book and some magazines for me to read on the way. The girls had intended to come to the docks with me but it was raining, so they did not come. I am rather glad that they did not, for it would have been unpleasant for them to go home alone from the docks.

The miner I have just been talking to, a man who came up on the *Pueblo* with me, is now bound for Dawson. My, but he has had some experiences in mining! He is thirty-six years old but does not look over twenty-eight or thirty. He has mined all over Alaska and the principal camps in the U.S. and also in Mexico. He has made lots of money, but like lots of others, has squandered it until he has nothing to show for all his years of hard work. He declares that he is going to save his money this time, but it is unlikely he will do so.

April 5, 1904

THE STATEROOM

Well, I am pretty comfortable in my stateroom. They could not give all the passengers bunks in the second-class part of the boat. So about eight or a dozen of us got staterooms. This is much better for me, as I can have a good bed, and take care of myself. This forenoon, I read *Darrel of the Blessed Isles* by Irvine Bachelor.

Edwin Warren

It is quite interesting, but I do not like it as well as *Dri and I.* I am not making much effort to see the scenery this trip, as it is too cold to be on deck much. I caught a cold somewhere, I think while on the *Pueblo,* and so I am taking the best care of myself that I can.

I got a small bottle of sweet oil in Seattle and also a bottle of cough medicine. I rub myself with the oil at night, and take the cough medicine quite often. I haven't coughed but a few times and I don't want to begin. I want to get over the cold before leaving the boat, if possible. I am going to take just as good care of myself as I can this trip.

April 6, 1904

WE MET THE STEAMER *PORTLAND*

My cold is somewhat better this morning, for which I am thankful. We passed Queen Charlotte Sound in the night. The rolling of the ship woke me up. Most of the way, the boat rides as smoothly as if on a river. There are only a few places that we cross open water. The weather is fine and has been throughout the trip. I am quite surprised we are not getting either snow or rain most of the time.

The food we get on this boat is pretty poor. I had made up my mind to let both tea and coffee entirely alone while away this summer, but I just about have to take a cup of coffee for breakfast, as it is about the only thing I can besides the bread and butter.

The mush is cooked in a thick, sticky mass, about as palatable as so much glue. We are getting up into the snow belt now. Nearly all the hills have snow on them, in patches. The tugboat pilot has just passed, having in tow one of the Treadwell's bulks loaded with suppurates, bound for the smelter in Tacoma. I don't see why they don't operate a smelter of their own at Treadwell; they have such an enormous output of ore.

[Treadwell did later operate their own smelter, just as Edwin thought they should.]

One of the fellows who has a berth in this stateroom just came in with a can of baked beans, which he had got a hold of somewhere onboard, and we had quite a feast on them. I had been rather puzzled as to what the nationality of this fellow was. He talks like an Irishman, but in appearance, was rather more like a Swede. I did not like to ask what country he was from, so finally was inspired to ask his name. "Pat Hahey," he said. That settled it conclusively.

There are four of us in this room; one is a young Finlander only ten months away from the old country, but still he speaks and understands English pretty well. Better, I think, than I could speak a foreign language in a ten-month stay in the country. We have passed a couple of pretty little lighthouses today. [I guess that they are] British by the white body and red top. This is still English territory, but we will cross Dixon's Entrance and be in Alaskan waters sometime tonight. I have been reading most of the day in the book Merle gave me for Christmas, entitled *The Pleasures of Life*, by Sir John Lubbock. It is a fine book full of noble and helpful thoughts. I am very glad I brought it with me. Well, it is nearly time for the first call to supper, and I think I will go and try for the first table, so as to have things hot, as they will probably be more palatable. I have had supper, such as it was, and I am now going to bed. We just met a large, nice-looking steamer, the *Portland*, which is on the Valdez run. It is almost like running into a friend to meet a boat up here.

April 7, 1904

BOWS AND ARROWS

Just leaving Ketchikan, we were in about three hours. I went onshore three times in hope of seeing Elmer Capp, but the stores were not open, so [I] missed him. I finally managed to get into one little store and buy a couple of lemons. I borrowed a cup and a spoon and some sugar from the steward, and got some hot water from the cook and made a big cup of hot lemonade, as I thought it would be good for my cold. Besides, I wanted something that would taste good. I'm not usually very fussy about my food, but it is about all I can do to eat anything they serve on this boat. It is mostly in the cooking, I think. There is no taste to anything, and the stuff is about half cold by the time you get it.

It is about [a] seventeen-hour run from Ketchikan to Douglas, so we will be getting in there late tonight or early tomorrow morning. The vibration from the machinery makes it about as hard to write as on a railway train, so I will read awhile, for a change. At Ketchikan, an Indian came on board with some bows and arrows for sale. The arrows, he said, were for grouse shooting, and were different from any I had seen before. They were not pointed at all, but the ends were very blunt and heavy.

They would kill a grouse easily enough without marking it, but I suspect it would take a native Indian to hit anything with it. We arrived at Petersburg at five PM. This is nothing but a big fish cannery with a small Swash village. It is situated at the lower end of Wrangle Narrows, which are fine fishing grounds, and owing to the abundance of fish, sea fowl are plentiful and the abundance of both birds and fish induce several pairs of bald eagles to make their residence here. I could see a couple of big nests not far from the cannery, and several of the majestic old eagles were seen in the vicinity. I don't think that they have begun to occupy the nests yet. Flocks of surf scooters were quite numerous, as were also pigeon guillemots, violet green cormorants, gulls, and ducks of various species. I heard one of the sailors inform a passenger, who was questioning him, that the scooters, which he called black divers, were very good eating, as were also the gulls.

April 8, 1904

THE FERRY *LONE FISHERMAN*

6:30 PM, Juneau, Alaska: I am writing this on board the little ferry boat, the *Lone Fisherman*, which is lying at the dock. My luggage is on board and I am bound for Treadwell. The boat does not cross till 8 o'clock, so I have got quite a little time to wait. The *Dolphin* got into Douglas at 3 AM, but I did not care to go ashore at that time of the night, as long as I had a good bed on the boat, and could just as well stay on board until we get to Juneau in the morning.

It will only cost me twenty-five cents to go from here to Treadwell, baggage and all, where if I had landed at Douglas in the night, I would have had to pay fifty cents for a bed, and then have to carry my things clear to Treadwell in the morning. It is raining steadily this morning, with occasionally a few flakes of snow, but it is not nearly as cold as when I left here in the middle of November.

The *Dolphin* is just pulling out for the run to Skagway, and I am glad I've seen the end of my voyage on her. For the modest sum of thirty cents, I was able to eat a couple of fried eggs and a cup of chocolate, with bread and potatoes, at a restaurant in Juneau this morning. They tasted good after being on steamer fare.

Chapter Five:
Return to Treadwell

April 11, 1904

THE THREE HUNDRED STAMP MILL

I went to work in the Three Hundred Stamp Mill the night of the eighth, which was right after I got here. I saw the foreman, Mr. Brown, and asked for work, but he told me that he had a full crew. I had already told Mr. Watson that I was going to try for a job in the mill. Later in the day, he came to me and said that he had been talking to Brown about me, and that Brown had said that he would give me a job if I knew anything about feeding. Mr. Watson told me to go and have a talk with him again, so I did, with the result that he hired me after waiting a while to see if another man for whom he had sent should come. Met George Gibson, who is now shift boss, and he offered to help me out in any way that he could. Also saw James Loussborogh, the assistant foreman. He told me I could have the job of cage tender at any time. The mill has been shut down entirely or only running a small number of stamps ever since the first night I worked, so I have been laid off ever since.

Treadwell 300 Stamp Mill
PCA - 230 - 11 Alaska State Library
Arthur C. Pillsbury creator

300 Mill, Vanner room
PCA - 39 - 0924
Alaska State Library
Case & Draper creators

Edwin Warren

April 14, 1904

A BEAUTIFUL AFTERNOON

I am setting on the back steps of the Bear's Nest boarding house, waiting for supper which comes at five, and then at twenty minutes past five. I have to commence my night's work in the mill. I have been working for several nights now, and am getting along pretty well. I will be glad though to get on day shift, as then, we won't have to work such hours on night shift, [where] we begin at 5:20 PM and work till 6:20 AM—thirteen hours. This is a beautiful afternoon, bright and clear, with the water in the channel as calm and still as in a sheltered lake. The mountains on the other side are covered with snow, but patches of the mountainside are beginning to show through.

April 16, 1904

A REMINDER OF PACIFIC GROVE

I am waiting for breakfast; this is change day, so I will only get a short sleep. There was a steamer came in last night about midnight. I think it was the *Cottage City,* as she was using a searchlight to make the landing. I expect a letter but I won't be able to get it until noon. Last night, my partner in the mill—that is, the feeder who works on the same side that I do—came up to me and started to get acquainted.

He had a piece of chalk, with which he wrote on the ore box. His first move was to write his name, David Ramsey, and the word, "Scotch," denoting his nationality. Then he wrote "Irish" which he applied to me, to this, I vigorously shook my head, and taking the chalk, I wrote my name for him. He seems to be a good-natured fellow, always ready to help you or show you anything you don't understand.

5:30 PM: Well, I got my letter from Merle that I have been wanting; it was a nice, cheery letter that did me a whole lot of good. She enclosed a little pressed buttercup, a reminder of the bright wildflowers of Pacific Grove at this season.

April 19, 1904

HE WAS PRETTY BADLY USED UP

Another day's work finished, and I will now have a few hours to call my own. I started to write this outside, but a few drops of rain fell on the page, warning me to go inside. The men are setting on the benches or standing around the room, waiting patiently for the dining room doors to swing open. A couple of newsboys have a lot of papers displayed for sale, so I suppose a boat most have come in from the south.

The newsboys are a pretty good sign of when to go to the post office, but I don't expect anything for a few days yet. I just met a man who was injured by falling rocks last fall while I was here. He was pretty badly used up; several bones broken, and he had to spend several months in the hospital. He has just begun work again, and looks quite pleased to be over his long idleness.

I believe that if I had been as nearly finished in the mine as he was, I would give it the go by in all future time, but I suppose the poor fellow doesn't know anything but mining. Supper is over and I am home at the Bear's Nest boarding house, which is what this bunk house is called.

I have just done a small washing, that is, my underwear and handkerchief. Now, I am going to enjoy a couple of hours' reading. My roommate has quite a stack of more-or-less recent magazines, and I can find a good many interesting articles in them. Last night, I started to read the book of Isaiah, and read six chapters.

I am much less familiar with the books of prophecy, than with historical parts of the bible. A couple of the boys whom I know are starting tonight for Atlin. I should almost like to go with them. Last summer, I planned to go there when I came up north, but having got started to work at the Treadwell, decided to stay the summer out. I do not expect to have a long enough season in Alaska this year to pay me to go to the interior.

April 21, 1904

FLOCKS OF GULLS ON THE BEACH

The flocks of gulls are constantly on the beach and swimming in or circling over the water. [They] are a mystery to me. They are of two distinct sizes; the larger one evidently being the glaucous-winged gull, but I can't satisfy myself as to the identity of the smaller ones. They are about the size of kittiwakes, but lack the black markings on the head and neck. They may be the short-billed gull, which is about that size. I will have to find out before I go back to Pacific Grove in order to satisfy myself. These flocks of beautiful white gulls add greatly to the scenery, giving it a touch of life and motion. When the water in the channel is calm, as it is just now, a gull swimming on the surface leaves a long wake behind in the deep water.

April 23, 1904

CHRISTIAN ENDEAVORS, THE FRIENDS' CHURCH

My most convenient time for writing in my diary seems to be while waiting for supper. I had to get a big move on myself; we leave the mill about twenty minutes past five, and as supper does not come until six, the interval furnishes a good chance for writing. Last night, I rushed from work right up to my room, and shaved myself before supper. I had to get a big move on myself, and when I came downstairs, I asked a fellow the time and he said just six; the whistle has just blown.

That meant late to supper and maybe I could not get a place at the table, so I started for the boarding house on the run. I got there pretty well out of breath, but just in time to join the rush into the dining room. After supper, went home, and after reading a short time, changed my clothes and went to the "Christian Endeavor" meeting at the Friends' Church.

The meeting was just commencing as I got here, but when it was over, I was given a warm welcome by my old friends; most of those who used to attend were present. The Methodist minister, Mr. Peterson, was present with his wife and children, and when I told him I was a Methodist, he invited me to come to his church, and when I told him where I was working, he said he would come up and see me. Mr. Jackson, the minister at the Friends' church, wants me to continue coming there.

I hardly know where to go, as I suppose I ought to attend the Methodist church, but I am acquainted at the Friends, and the members have been very kind to me. Perhaps the best way to fix it up will be to attend the Sunday evening preaching service at the Methodist and then go to the Christian Endeavor at the Friends' church on Friday night. A gentleman and his wife from Juneau, who are in mission work, led the meeting and both talked very earnestly.

I was introduced to them, but as usual, I gave all notice to the folks themselves, and little thought to the name, so consequently did not remember it. That is a fault of mine that I most overcome. It was moonlight coming home and a beautiful night it was; along the shore was a bright strip of water. While further out the shadows of the mountains across the channel darkened the water, even then the reflection of the snow-filled gullies on the mountainside could be plainly seen in the glassy surface. Juneau nestling in a cove at the base of a rather high, snow-topped mountain, made its position known by scores of lights, the lower ones sending bright rays across the water. The entire range of mountains on the opposite side was plainly visible, the moon illuminating the snowy mountain summits. The air was still and cool, and "every breath fills you with the joy of living."

Edwin Warren

April 26, 1904

THE FRIENDS' CHURCH

Well, time does go by somehow; it is as if I have written in this diary just about every day, but here it is three days since the last entry. The Bear's Nest where I hang up my hat and call home is but a few yards from one end of the mill, so when my work was over for the day, I ran over and climbed up the ladder which is fastened to the side of the building, and crawled through the open window and was in my room in very short order. The reason for this course of action is a light rain, which made me think my umbrella would be a good thing to carry when I go up to supper, so I am putting in a few minutes with my pencil before starting for the boarding house. Sunday night, I went to church at the Friends, as I concluded to go where I am acquainted. Yesterday noon I went to the post office on my way to dinner and got letters from home and from Merle. I ate a very hasty meal, then went out into the waiting room and had time to read them both before going back to the mill. In the evening, after reading over the letters a time or two, I sat down and answered them both. I felt in a good mood for writing and managed to write answers to them of respectable length. Well, I must get a move on, and get out of here or I will be late for supper.

April 27, 1904

THE BEAUTY OF INDIAN CANOE

Just a month since I left Pacific Grove; it seems much longer, though. This is Saturday afternoon and I am sitting on a log upon the bluff beyond the Douglas cemetery, nearly opposite Juneau. It is a pleasant, warm day, about the best we have had for some time. Owing to the snow with which we have had lately, the water is low and half the mill is shut down.

PCA - 39 - 0887 Alaska State Library
Treadwell Glory hole
Case & Draper creators

So I had to take a day off. It may be several days off for all I know. That is one trouble with that 300 mill: If it happens to be a dry season, you will lose enough time to lower your wages considerable. It has other drawbacks too, and I don't like the job any too well. Long hours and the constant noise and jar make it rather disagreeable; still I'm standing the work all right, and I suppose I ought not to complain. The main trouble is I have to work under a very cranky and impatient sort of man. But of course, it is hard for him to get along with green men, and is probably as great a trial to put up with my ignorance of mill work, as it is for me to put up with his impatience.

I have been thinking of quitting and going to work at the mine for a while, but I guess I will try and stand it where I am for a while. It seems hard to realize that I am on an island, and this beautiful strip of water below me is part of the Pacific Ocean. True, it has the deep blue color of the ocean, and more of the ocean's stillness, and yet it seems more like a splendid river. Lying here between these mountain ranges as in a beautiful valley, except that the forest-covered mountains rise directly from the water's edge.

A long, slender Indian canoe is just passing below me containing a couple of men, four women, and several young ones. The women have on red shawls, and different colored head cloths, and look quite picturesque as they paddle along. Oh yes, the women are doing their share of the paddling, as I guess they do of everything else. Still the men are rather industrious; a good many of them are working at the Treadwell.

They won't work underground, but work in the big open pit called the glory hole; as one Indian told me, they want to be able to see the sky over their heads. Not a bad idea either, as there is not much danger of any portion of the sky dropping down on you.

Looking up the channel from where I am sitting, the mountains seem rather low and heavily forested, while to the south, they are higher, with more rugged peaks, and more snow. A high mountain capped by three mountain peaks, seems to block the channel, but I suppose like a river the water winds around its base.

A flock of surf ducks are floating quietly in the channel below, and an occasional gull swings idly past. Otherwise bird life seems very scarce; there are a few ravens about, and I can hear one of them croaking nearby, as I write about him. At intervals through the afternoon, I have been hearing a dull, booming sound back in the hills. It must be the noise made by the male grouse, although I never heard it before. Some of the surf ducks are flying now, and by the large white spot on each wing I know them to be the white-winged scoter.

More Indians are passing, this time in a rowboat; they don't look as picturesque as the others did in the genuine Indian canoe. A very graceful craft is their canoe, long and narrow, it stands quite high out of the water, and the ends are raised into, high sharp prows, often with an eagle or such emblem carved on them.

APRIL 27, 1904

RESCUING A LITTLE INDIAN BOY

As I was returning along the track near the sawmill, I heard a lusty squalling ahead of me. It proceeded from a little Indian boy who seems to be in trouble of some kind. I ran up to him as fast as I could, and found that he had fallen through a sort of broken platform and was hanging there by the neck. His head above and body below the planks, he could partly support his weight by hanging on with his little fists, but would have been in a pretty bad fix if somebody hadn't happened along soon. I lifted him out and looked him over but did not find any serious injuries, then I happened to think of a bag of peanuts which I had just bought in town; so, pulling out a handful, I offered them to him. It worked like magic. The noise ceased and the fat, dirty, puckered-up face became calm and serene. I left him fully cured.

APRIL 27, 1904

INDIAN BEAR HUNTERS

A little farther along the track, I came to a shack in front of which a man was scraping sawdust over the inside of a huge bearskin. He had shot the bear about a week ago on Admiralty Island, a large island south of here, which is a great place for game. I got the man, who seemed quite talkative, to telling some of his hunting experiences; he says that these bears are very dangerous beasts to hunt and that one man should never go for them alone; a good many hunters, both Indians and white men have been killed by them.

Two men had been killed within a mile of where he shot this bear. They had no trouble getting this one, as he was in his hole, and they smoked him out, shooting him as he emerged. He told of one man who was treed by a wounded bear, and kept at the top of the tree stub for a day and a half, the

Edwin Warren

bear finally giving it up and leaving him. Once he was hunting there with another fellow, and they saw two old bears, with a couple of cubs.

They were on a steep mountainside, and he told his partner not to shoot, as the hides were not in good condition and the old bears would put up a mean fight, having the cub. They got separated and pretty soon he heard a couple of shots, followed by a great shouting and commotion in the bush on the side of the mountain. He made what speed he could to the scene, and when nearly there, saw his partner on top of a rock with the old bears getting close up to him. Taking quick aim, he fired and dropped one bear.

The second shot went through his friend's coat and shirt, and just grazed his shoulder, but didn't injure him. Another shot downed the other bear. His friend was safe after a pretty close call. The Indians now have good guns for bear hunting, but formerly, when they had old-fashioned, unreliable guns they would go after bear in quite a large company. When they had found the game, they would all take careful aim, probably from several sides, all fire at once, and then make a rush pell-mell for their canoes, every man for himself. Arriving at their canoes, they would not wait to see results, but would paddle home and return the next day and look for the dead bear. If their volley had been successful, they would find the carcass somewhere near, but if not, well, the beast would have probably taken himself off. They know better than to wait with empty guns for a wounded bear to charge on them. These bears, the man told me, often go in bands; he said that five or six was not an uncommon number to find together, and he said that an Indian once told him that he had seen fourteen large bears in one band. They are mostly brown bears, but a few grizzlies are in the country.

He said that a good hide like the one he was working on, was worth forty to sixty dollars when properly cured; it was certainly a fine skin with thick, long, fine hair. It has been a quiet restful Sabbath for me. I did not get up until after seven o'clock, so missed breakfast. The forenoon I spent in reading read half a dozen chapters of Isaiah, then the last few chapters of Merle's book. Had a very good dinner as usual on Sundays, consisting of clam chowder soup, roast beef, mashed potatoes, canned corn, boiled cabbage, rye bread, cheese, and milk.

THE DOUGLAS SALOON
PCA - 39 - 0802 Alaska State Library
W. H. Case creator

May 1, 1904

THE DOUGLAS SALOON

 After dinner, I took a walk down the track in the opposite direction from the way I went yesterday. Passed a row of Indian shacks in front of which were long strips of fish drying on poles. In front of one cabin was a long line of seaweed drying. It was a peculiar kind, in bunches, and at a distance might be taken for bunches of dried grapes. I followed the track to the end, and then got on a trail which led along the hillside among the timber.

I over took three boys who were hunting with small rifles and walked a ways with them. One of them was the son of Joseph McDonald, the general superintendent of Treadwell Co. The trail wound about over fallen logs and around trees and stumps. For a short distance, it followed a flume in which a couple of inches of water were running, and in which were large blocks of ice. Soon we came to a solid log cabin which had been occupied by some miners who were working a prospect nearby, but which now was deserted. As we followed the trail around the mountain, we soon came to the abandoned tunnel on which the prospectors had wasted their time, labor, and money.

We saw another place where a shaft had been sunk; it was nearly full of water. It must have been a good many years since it had been worked, as the cabins were all in ruins. The woods were very quiet and pretty; no grass or wildflowers have sprung up yet, but everywhere on the ground where tree trunks had fallen, logs were covered with a velvety growth of bright green moss. The boys were going further than I wanted to take the time to go, so I left them and came back home. This is payday, and I will have to go up to the office directly and see if there is anything coming to me. My wages from the fifteenth until the first will be retained in the office until I quit work, so I will only have from the eighth to the fifteenth, and I lost three days out of that.

Then there is the hospital and gymnasium fees, and store bill to be deducted. I will not get much this time. Tonight there is to be a grand opening of a saloon in Douglas. It is being started by a man who has been a blacksmith at Treadwell for a long time. He is a very jolly, witty fellow, an Irishman well-liked by the men. That will be so much the worse, as they will probably patronize his place more freely. He had a good job, about four dollars a day and board, and it seems a pity he should give that up to go into the business of helping his friends to get down and stay down. Judge Irwin, a remarkable old man who used to speak occasionally at the YMCA, is to give a talk at the Methodist church tonight. They have got out placards announcing the meeting, probably in the hopes of attracting some of the men from the grand opening. But it is highly improbable if many of them could be induced to attend church in place of the other event. Six thirty PM: Drew my pay which amounted to five dollars and five cents.

I started up to the office about half past four, and on the way saw Mr. Brown, the foreman of the mill. He said I was just the man he was looking for and told me that McClellan, the foreman of the Mexican mine, wanted to see me. Said he thought he wanted to put me to work, so I went up and found McClellan outside the mill, so had no difficulty in talking to him.

He explained that his night shift oilier was sick and that he had left word for another man to come and take the job, but did not know whether he would show up or not. He told me to come up after supper, and if the other fellow was not there, he would give me the place, the Mexican mine. So I hurried back and got supper, then came to my room and put on my old clothes, then went to the three hundred mill, where I have been working, to get my overalls and jumper. Saw Brown and told him that I did not know whether I was going to work. He then explained that one of his old amalgamators, an experienced man who had worked for him in previous seasons, had returned and he had given him my place as feeder. However, he said that if I didn't get a job at the Mexican mine, to come back the next day and he would put me to work at some extra work that would take perhaps two weeks. Went up to the Mexican mine and found that the other man was there, but the foreman told me that he might be able to give me a steady job before too long.

May 2, 1904

THE STEAMER *COTTAGE CITY*

The *Cottage City* came in during the night, brought me a letter from Merle, which I lost no time in answering in order that it may go back on the same boat. Saw Brown this morning, and he told me to come to work this afternoon. Last night, went to the Friends' church; there were only two adults and one little girl present, besides the minister and family, and myself. Probably most of the churchgoers, and they are few enough, had gone to hear Judge Irwin. I asked Mr. Jackson if he had any books, and he told me to look over the small library belonging to the Junior Endeavors.

I did not see much that interested me, but finally took one of Florence M. Kingsley's books, entitled *Paul the Herald of the Cross*. I have read several chapters in it, and it promises to be quite interesting.

I had hoped to get acquainted with some of the great essayists this summer, as I know some of their works used to be in the Treadwell library. Ruskin especially I have been hoping to read, also Carlyle. In fact, I would be glad to get hold of almost any of the standard English authors, essayists, or poets, in order that my reading may be of value in getting a good foundation in English literature.

May 4, 1904

FINDING FOSSILS ON DOUGLAS ISLAND

It is raining steadily today, so I am laying off. My present job is outside work at the mill, but I did not think it would pay me to work in the rain and be soaking wet all day, so did not go to work this morning. Yesterday I gathered a pocket full of fossil shells, from the sides and bottom of small water course, where it was cutting down through a gravel bank, a hundred yards or so back from the channel.

I had supposed that these coast islands were formed by the submergence of the land, and probably that is the case, but these fossil shells show that this particular part has been raised from the sea. I do not know whether fossils are to be found higher up on the island or not.

Saw a small flock of juncos, but they were so much tawnier-colored, and were so light-colored on the head that I scarcely knew them. I almost thought they were sparrows at first, but when they flew, the white tail feathers removed all doubt of their identity. Birds, except ravens and Northwest crows and the gulls on the beach, are not at all common.

A small number of robins were seen out near the cemetery, and there is occasionally a bald eagle, or a pair of them to be seen, but aside from these I have not seen many birds. I saw a little warbler of some kind last Sunday, when I was out in the woods, and heard one or two others singing.

From what I hear, grouse are fairly plentiful higher up among the timber, and ptarmigans are taken in the winter up among the snow-covered summits. I have never seen a hawk or any kind of a bird of prey up here except the eagles. There is a small island in the channel near here called Juneau Island; on it are a number of scrubby trees and one or two good-sized snags. Very often, I can see the black outlines of an old eagle perched on one of the snags, the conspicuous white head and tail showing up as plain as lights on a dark night. I had a talk with Dave Ramsay this morning while waiting for breakfast. He was my partner in the mill, a great big strapping Scotch lad, I had often thought how easy it must be for him to do a day's work which I would consider hard. But he tells me that he is troubled with pleurisy so bad sometimes that he can't sleep, and last fall he had his knee injured and had to spend four months in the hospital.

So he has his own troubles, and I am not inclined to envy him his bulk. This afternoon, the rain let up and I went down to Douglas to call on the Jacksons. Mr. Jackson was not at home; his wife told me that he had gone down the channel in his launch after some logs. He had purchased some lumber from the sawmill for his schoolhouse, and was to make payment in logs.

The logs were some that had drifted on Admiralty Island. By towing these up to the mill, he would be able to save a good deal on his lumber bill. He owns a small launch, which he uses in his mission work. Mrs. Jackson told me that the Friends have two other missions in Alaska beside the one here, one at Kake Island, south of here, and one way up in Kotzebue Sound, within the Arctic Circle. The work among the natives

Edwin Warren

at this place is more difficult than at the other missions, owing to the degenerating influence the white man has over the Indians—furnishing them drink and debauching them generally.

A difficulty also exists, she says, in there being missions of several different denominations here. The natives who profess Christianity take advantage of this, and if remonstrated with for not living right, will go and join some other church. She says that it is much easier to keep up the standard of living, where there is but one denomination. As I was leaving, she brought out a very good pair of field glasses to see if Mr. Jackson's boat was in sight.

We could see a boat with a sail several miles down the channel, and she said that he sometimes used a sail on the launch, but at that distance, she could not tell whether it was his boat or not.

She pointed out their schoolhouse on the other side, where the mission has a grant of land four miles in length along the shore; they are in hopes to get a colony of Indians established there in time, and so get them by themselves and away from the whites. Tonight I ate supper in the big dining room, among the Slovenians, for a change. They are rather a fierce-looking crowd, and in different garb they might pass easily enough for the Balkan Banditti of which we so often see pictures. They are almost all cigarette smokers, a very clannish set they are, and it is just as well, as none of the other men would mix with them.

They are not much given to drinking in the downtown saloons, but almost anytime you take a walk down the track, you will meet several of them packing big demijohns of liquor home with them. Last summer, I got to know several of the younger Slavs pretty well, and they seemed to be rather good-natured, easygoing fellows.

The one of them who I knew best, Yek Perovich, is not here now, at least I have not seen him, although his younger brother is still here. He was quite a bright young fellow, big and well-built, and would have been really handsome in good clothes. It was his ambition to become an American. One night I met him downtown, and he wanted to take me into a saloon and treat me. When I told him I didn't drink, he seemed quite dumbfounded, and looked at me like he had never seen a specimen of that kind before. He asked me how I could live without drinking, and I told him I got along first rate without it, better than most folks do with it. This is Wednesday night and the friends have a prayer meeting somewhere, I don't know whether at the church or at a private house, may go downtown and try to find it after awhile if it does not rain.

The *Humboldt* came up the channel as I was going to supper, but don't suppose she has brought me anything, except maybe a roll of papers, but I will be glad of that even. Today I finished *Paul a Herald of the Cross,* and also completed the book of Isaiah, besides reading about a dozen chapters in Proverbs. Bill Piper has just came in from work, bringing one of E.P. Roe's books with him, which he has borrowed somewhere; the title is *Without a Home.* I may read it if I get a chance.

May 6, 1904

MONTHLY CLEANUP IN THE MILL

The monthly cleanup in the mill is going on now. It lasts about twelve days, and consists of removing the amalgam and gold from the plates, and putting in new stamps and dies. To remove the gold from the plates, they have to be heated; they are about five feet wide by eight feet long, and placed on an incline. The crushed ore is carried down then by rinsing water, and the gold is taken up by the amalgam on the plates.

A wooden cover is placed over the plate, and sacks put over all crevices. Then a big steam hose is turned on under the cover, and the heating process begins, after being steamed for about half an hour, the cover is removed, and the surface of the plate is scraped with sharp chisels.

The scrapings are a mixture of gold and quicksilver, and have to be heated to get them apart. When sufficient heat is applied, the quicksilver is vaporized, and the gold left. When cool, the quicksilver can be collected again.

Edwin Warren

May 7, 1904

NO MORE SUNDAY WORK

This is Saturday evening; I quit work at noon today, in order to draw my wages tonight. I have been impressed that it is wrong for me to continue to work here where Sunday work is required. Everything runs full-blast on Sunday, the same as any other day, and if you work at all, you have got to do the Sunday labor, whether you want to or not.

But the point is just this: I am not forced to work here, and if I do so, I am accepting the Sunday work in order to make more money, and that is clearly wrong. So I am going to start south in a very short time. I will get back to Pacific Grove in just about time to get a good job for the summer. Last night, I asked Mr. Jackson if he had ever noticed any bald eagles' nests when he had been out with his boat.

He said, "Yes, I know where there is a couple, and the birds are sitting now," but he seemed to think it would be a very dangerous job to try to get the eggs. He had heard of a man getting killed trying to rob a nest, also an Indian was attacked so fiercely at another nest that he had to give it up. I am going to try and get him to take me to the nest with his boat the first of the week. I called at his house to see him this afternoon, but he was absent, calling on some of the natives, his wife told me. She told me of an old eagle that had been hanging around the timber up on the hills above their house. She had taken a shot at him with a rifle, and must have come pretty close to him, as he flew before the sound could have reached him.

They thought that he might have a nest somewhere back in the hills, so while I was waiting for Mr. Jackson to come, I thought I would have a look for it. I followed a trail up a little stream for a ways, then up through the woods, and out on to an open space where the ground was covered with a soft, wet, spongy growth of moss.

But neither eagles nor their nests were to be seen. I had hardly expected to find a nest so far back from the channel, for they generally build close to the water. However, I had a pleasant walk; after the trail crossed the open, it again entered the woods, and soon came out at the edge of quite a deep canyon along the side of which it ran, reminding me of the trails and canyons down in the Sur County below Monterey. After wandering around for a couple of hours, I made my way back to the Jackson home, but he had not returned.

Mrs. Jackson said that he would have service at the Indian chapel at 8 PM, so I agreed to be there at that time. It is very doubtful if these bald eagles are any more inclined to fight for their eggs than the golden eagles are; some people have an idea that all eagles are very fierce around their nests, but this is not the case with the golden eagle, and if Mr. Jackson will give me a chance, I will soon find out for myself how the white-headed birds will act.

May 8, 1904

THE INDIAN CHURCH

Last night, I attended at the native chapel. About twenty-five adult Indians and a good many children were present, and the meeting was much more lively and interesting than any I have attended among the white people. Mr. Jackson said that he was planning a trip to Taku Harbor in his launch on Monday or Tuesday; he suggested that I accompany him. Today I attended Sunday school at the church in the forenoon, preaching to the natives in the afternoon, and am going to service at the church tonight. I stayed all night at the Jacksons' last night, and took breakfast with them this morning. The home cooking tasted good. The meetings for the natives are by far better attended than those of the white churches.

The Indians seem to take quite an interest, and sing and testify with a great deal of earnestness. Mr. Jackson says that they sometimes switch off and go to talking about the meanness of their neighbors, or some other topic which is not usually the subject of a testimony in a religious meeting.

Still they have some good, faithful ones upon whom they can depend. Bill Arthur, the powder man, with whom I worked last summer, told me tonight that he did not want to see me go away now, as he thought that in a couple of weeks there would be a chance for me to go on with him again. He said that he would rather have me with him on the job than any other man up here.

It's not a bad job, either, all day shift and light work, with no interference from anyone, and is about the only job I would take in the mine. But you have to work on Sunday, as with all other work here, and I am through with Sunday labor, unless it is something necessary. Bill is a very nice fellow to work with, but he will soon ruin himself with disseveration if he keeps on the way he is going.

MAY 10, 1904

TAKU HARBOR WITH REV. JACKSON

Well, I am all packed up, and ready for the *City of Seattle* when she stops at Douglas on her way down from Skagway to Seattle. I had a splendid day yesterday; went with Mr. Jackson to Taku harbor, twenty-five miles from here, in his gasoline motor launch, the *Hooney*. We started from Douglas about nine AM. It was nice and clear and the channel very smooth.

When we got down by the end of Douglas Island, about eight miles from town, he said he would show me that eagle's nest that he had been telling me of. He ran in close to shore, and pointing to a thick bunch in the top of a spruce, said, "There it is." It did not take many minutes to see that he had mistaken a mass of thick branches for a nest. It is about five miles across from Douglas Island to Admiralty Island, but it did not take long to cross with the launch. We were then in one of the most dangerous places for navigating in Alaska, off the Taku Inlet. Heavy squalls come up very suddenly, the wind sweeping down the inlet like a hurricane. There also are very dangerous tide rips as they are called, where two tides meet. A good stiff breeze was blowing, and the water was quite choppy, but we put up the sail and went dancing over the chops at a good rate of speed. In about an hour, we were in smoother water, and as it was past noon, we ate our lunch.

Pretty soon, a mass of smoke which we had seen ahead of us evolved into a steamer, and before long, we met a large, nice-looking boat which we knew to be the *City of Seattle* on her up trip. Soon we rounded a point and made for the entrance to Taku Harbor. It is a rather small harbor, horseshoe-shaped, and surrounded by high forest-clad mountains. It is a very pretty place. There is a large cannery, fish saltery, and cold storage plant here.

They were preparing for the season's pack, putting their barrels and kegs together, and getting their cans ready. A good deal of the work of cutting out and putting the cans together is done by machinery attended by line men. The foreman took us through the cold storage plant, racks full of big salmon, and fine large salmon trout frozen as hard as rocks.

These are sent to Seattle on a refrigerator boat. We bought a loaf of bread, some cookies, and a can of salmon and a pound of raisins at the cook house for provisions for the trip back to Douglas. Mr. Jackson had brought a big bundle of papers, which he left with the lady at the cook house. She seemed very glad to see a minister; she said that they were Episcopalians.

While we were at the cannery, a very heavy squall came up. The wind blew with great velocity and the water was rough and stormy in almost no time. I was glad we were in a good safe place, and not out in the channel. It did not last long, though, but was followed by rain. I thought that we were going to have a rough trip home, but it cleared up about the time we were ready to start.

As we were going out of the harbor, I saw a bald eagle fly to a nest in a big spruce or fir tree a short distance back from the shore. Of course, I was anxious to stop and go to it, but it was then half past three, and Mr. Jackson was afraid it would make us too late if we stopped, as it would take us till night to get home, at best, and if it should be rough, we would need all our time. So we had to leave it, and I saw only one or two other nests on the way, but did not stop.

We had enough wind to sail for a ways, but it gradually went down, and we had to depend on the engine. That took us along at a pretty good speed, though once in a while, it would balk, but a few minutes' tinkering would put it all right again. We kept close inshore most of the way back, to avoid the tide rips, and had very smooth water most of the way. Jackson showed me a cliff or precipice on the side of a mountain rising from the water, from which the Indians gather gulls' eggs by using a long rope. Looking up Taku Inlet, we could see a series of sharp, jagged mountain peaks, snow-covered and with glaciers on their sides.

They belong to the Rocky Mountains, he told me as here the Rockies and the coast range come close together. After crossing the inlet, we again followed the shore. We saw Grindstone Falls, a beautiful cascade surrounded by green forest. The scenery was superb; the water was as smooth as glass and the green-forested snow-topped mountains were reflected in the water very clearly.

We passed Taku Indian village, a very pretty little place with a couple of large potlatch houses or temples. There was quite a large burying ground nearby, each grave surmounted by a tiny house; one of them, the grave of a chief, being a very fancy structure, nicely painted.

MAY 10, 1904

A CANOE FOR THE AFTERLIFE

Every now and then, we would see an Indian grave along the shore, on the bank. In most cases, the dead man's canoe was to be seen beside the grave, where it had been placed for his future use, when he was buried. We saw a good many ducks and scoters, and quite a few other sea birds, especially murrelets, guillemots, murres, loons, and cormorants, together with the ever-present gulls; also saw a flock of small gulls with black heads, which I took to be Bonaparte's. Some of the chicks were very pretty; I think there were some eiders among them. The scenery was superb, the water was as smooth as glass, and the green-forested, snow-topped mountains were reflecting in the water very clearly.

INDIAN BURIAL GROUNDS

Mr. Jackson had brought along an old muzzle-loading musket and some powder and shot, but he failed to bag any ducks, although we had some good shots. I laid the blame on the musket, as I believe I could have got something with my shotgun. Jackson maintained that the musket was a good shooting gun, but I noticed there was nothing more to gather up after his shots than after mine.

I had to laugh at some of his identifications; we saw a loon in the water, and he insisted that it was a goose. Later, a couple of loons passed us on wing, and these he pronounced mallards or ganos backs, I have forgotten which. We got back to the vicinity of the Treadwell about eight o'clock, and as there was a meeting in one of the Indian cabins on the beach, we went ashore, tied up the boat, and went to the meeting.

While he was tying up the boat, I ran over to the post office and got a couple of letters, which the *Seattle* had brought up. After the meeting, we took some passengers aboard and went up to Douglas. We put the people off at the Douglas Wharf, then took the launch up to the beach and anchored her where the outgoing tide would leave her dry, as he wanted to repair the rudder in the morning. Mr. Jackson took me home with him for the night, and after breakfast this morning, I took a walk down along the beach for about seven miles to see if I could not get a set of eagles' eggs, but no nests could be found. It was very hard walking, as the beach was covered nearly all the way with rocks and boulders of all sizes. One needs a boat to do any traveling in southwestern Alaska.

I got back to my room about three o'clock, and after eating some lunch, packed up my things, as I wanted to get everything into my telescope bag and not have two bundles. I discarded all the things that I did not really need to bring home, and managed to get them all in the one bundle. Bill seemed to feel rather sore about my leaving; I suppose he dislikes changing roommates, not knowing who he will be having put in with him.

    The *City of Seattle* came back from Skagway earlier than I expected, and I did not have time to go up to Jackson's' as I had promised, but I stopped in at the Indian chapel, and found Mr. Jackson there as it was almost time for meeting. After bidding him good-bye, I went to the dock at Douglas, and before long the *Seattle* came over from Juneau and I got aboard.

Chapter Six:
From Treadwell Minor to Stanford Student

We left about nine thirty PM. It was not dark, however, and I stayed up on deck for a couple of hours, as it was a beautiful night and the lights and shadows on the water, and the clear-cut outlines of the mountains against the sky made a scene that I will not soon forget. For quite a distance in the channel near Taku Harbor, the water was full of phosphorescence. It did not show in the undisturbed water, but the waves rolling back from the prow of the boat were full of it, gleaming and sparkling with thousands of tiny lights.

May 11, 1904

TONKA INDIAN VILLAGE

The first thing I saw this morning as I walked on deck was an eagle's nest in a tall treetop. One of the old birds was perched nearby. We were in Wrangle Narrows, near Tonka. The boat stopped a few minutes at Tonka, and a lady had a crate brought on board, which contained three wild geese. During the forenoon, I saw a number of eagles' nests, some with the white-headed proprietor calmly reposing on them. We called in at Fort Wrangle, a pretty little town where there was previously a U.S. garrison. Indian squaws were squatting on the deck, with an array of baskets, moccasins, etc. for sale. There is quite an Indian village here, with several large totem poles in front of the houses. At Ketchikan, which we reached about 4 PM, I found Elmer Cap at the store where he is working. He has a pretty good job, and is looking as though the place agrees with him. He said it did him good to see someone from home. His folks are living in Seattle now; I got their address and will call on them if I get time.

We met the freight steamer *AL-KI* near Ketchikan, and we stopped and took on some papers from her. Just as we were casting off from the dock at Ketchikan, three or four Japanese men came on at a dead run, and throwing their bundles on the deck, jumped over the rail just as the boat was swinging off. A number of Indians that we had on board left us here. [*Al-Ki* later shipwrecked. Barry Kibler.]

May 12, 1904

BELLA BELLA INDIAN VILLAGE

We are crossing Queen Charlotte Sound; it is quite good weather and we are having a good trip. It has been cloudy and gloomy part of the day, so that we could not enjoy the scenery as well as if it had been clear, but still there has been enough to see. We passed a very picturesque Indian village about noon; it is called Bella Bella. The houses were well-built and painted, and a church and schoolhouse were in evidence. The *City of Seattle* is about the best boat I have traveled on yet. The accommodations are good, as is also the food. She has only a small crowd on this trip, and that makes a big difference. It is hard to get things to suit you on any of the boats when they are crowded.

9 PM: this has been a grand evening; the scenery is quite different now from what it was farther up. There is no snow to speak of except on the highest peaks.

The islands are flatter and not so rugged. The sunset was beautiful, the horizon all gold and crimson, and as the sun sank lower, the color was cast on the water in mellow patches of gold. We passed Port Simpson and Kingston about sundown; the latter place is a very pretty little settlement with a sawmill and cannery. Parties of young folks were out in a rowboat and they waved their hands as we passed them. The waves from the steamer made their boat rock quite hard. We just met the *Humboldt* on her north trip; she had a big crowd on board.

May 13, 1904

PORT OF VANCOUVER

1 PM: Dinner is just over; soon after we got up this morning, I noticed a familiar-looking lighthouse and other landmarks and knew we were nearing Vancouver. The water was light-colored, caused by the outflow of the Frazer River.

We got in to the dock about eight o'clock; the first mate told me that she would remain about a half hour, so I went uptown and got some oranges. It is a little less than a year since I was in Vancouver; I left here in June 1903 on the *Princess May*. I was sorry not to have the time to go around and see the sights of the town and park, as it is a nice, clear day. Still the harbor is pretty, and there is enough to see.

The *Danube,* a boat I went aboard here last June, came into the dock a few moments after we did. The *City of Seattle* is making good time down Puget Sound. We are passing points and islands, and cute little lighthouses in great variety. They say we will get to Seattle about eight o'clock tonight. That will be the quickest time in which I have made the trip.

May 14, 1904

PORT OF SEATTLE

Seattle, Washington: We got in here last night about seven o'clock. That was a very convenient time to land, as it gave me time to find a room, gets something to eat, and get my telescope up from the dock

Edwin Warren

before bedtime. The difference in temperature is as noticeable coming down as it was going up. It seems quite warm here to me; last night I could hardly go to sleep, and kicked the clothes off the bed before I got things cool enough to suit me. The *Centennial* is to sail for San Francisco tomorrow afternoon, and as she is the only boat going for several days, I have got my ticket to go on her. I got out of coming up on her, but it seems as though I can't manage to give her the slip both ways. I'd rather go on most any old boat, however, than lay around Seattle many days.

It is hard work at best, for me to bum around a city. I spent most of today in the public library, found some very interesting bird books, also looked through the reports of the Harriman Expedition to Alaskan scenery, some of which I have seen. One of the scientists of the expedition declared that the scenery of the Inside Passage is the finest of its kind in the world.

This afternoon, I took a ride out on the car past the University of Washington and Ravenna Park. The trees are all coming out in their new foliage, making things look very fresh and clean.

May 15, 1904

ABOARD CENTENNIAL

4 PM: On board *Centennial,* we left Seattle promptly at two o'clock. This is a rather large boat, but ungainly it seems to me; she is long and narrow, and quite low in the water. She has a good many passengers on board. I will not venture an opinion on the quality of the accommodations until after I have had an eat and a sleep on board. Last night I heard Col. French speak in the Salvation Army tent, and this morning listened to an address which he made to the members of the Plymouth Congregational Church. This is a warm, quiet day, very still on the sound. There were several steamers lying at the Seattle docks, preparing to sail for home.

The first of them goes in a few days, though June 1st is considered as early as it is safe for them to start, on account of the ice in the Bering Sea. The way that the men are rushing north this season, there will be the usual surplus of labor, and consequently a good many will see hard times before they get back to civilization. I noticed a jager flying over the water shortly before we reached the dock at Seattle last Friday night, also one or two farther up the sound.

I am sitting on the deck, writing; a Japanese man has just come and sat down beside me and is looking on very closely as I write. He is a very homely Japanese man; as he does not blush to see me write this plainly about his personal appearance, I presume he does not read English very readily. Perhaps he will come to it later on, if I was real sure he would understand it. I would write more about him, but I fear it would be wasted. He has just been trying to begin a conversation with me in Japanese, but I don't feel like talking just now and it is slightly chilly. We have several Japanese on board.

I heard some of the fellows telling that one of them felt his dinner coming up, and not having time to get to the side of the ship, took his hat off and used it for a washbasin, throwing it overboard with its load as soon as he reached the rail. I have been watching the crew sew canvas covers on big tin cans of hard tack, or ship's biscuits.

The ship's name is stenciled on the tins, and they are then lashed in the small boat, in case of a wreck. We passed Point Arena about noon; a large flock of petrels were resting in the water or flying around, about a couple of miles off the point. The coast is rather rugged and severe-looking along here; it was somewhere up here on this barren coast that Margaret was born. Well I'm glad that I wasn't born up here, or at least that I don't have to live here. The albatrosses, to the number of about a dozen, still follow the ship.

They all seem to belong to one species, being dark brown, nearly black, all over. There is one exception; one single bird has white tail coverts, and seems to be a little lighter colored on the body. I presume it belongs to another species. On looking up the subject in the Seattle

Library, I found that some of the ducks that Mr. Jackson and I saw the day we went to Taku Harbor were harlequins.

I am sorry I failed to secure some specimens, as they are very desirable. We are getting well out toward the Pacific; the water is still very calm, and the ship has no motion except the vibration from the engines. Parties of passengers are sitting up here on deck on a pile of lumber, singing "Aunt Dinah's Quilting Party", "The Spanish Cavaliers," and other familiar hymns. It is getting almost too dark to write. A beautiful snowy range of the Olympics are still plainly to be seen on the left, while on the right, but farther away, is the dark outline of Vancouver Island.

May 16, 1904

We are still out on the Pacific and no land is in sight. The boat is rolling quite heavily and a good many of the passengers are sick. I haven't felt very bad yet, but did not care to eat any breakfast. There are about a half dozen albatrosses following the ship this morning.

They are immense birds; with long narrow wings, their flight over the water is simply superb, and a sight well worth seeing. Very few gulls are around the boat this trip.

Last night, I saw several tufted puffins in the vicinity of Port Townsend. They were in fine plumage, with bright red beaks and long plumes. Marbled murrelet were quite common, mostly in pairs, and I saw one or two jagers.

There was a very pretty sunset on the sound last night. We did not stop at Victoria, but her lights were plainly seen as we passed. I went to bed before we got out of the straits, but long before morning, I was awakened by the rolling of the ship.

MAY 18, 1904

We are in sight of the California coast, and expect to make San Francisco late tonight. The water is pretty rough and the boat rolls heavily. I was sick most all day yesterday, and kept to my bunk, but felt better towards night and got up and ate some supper. In the evening, I sat up on deck till rather late.

A lighthouse, or rather the light, was in sight for a long time. It was a revolving light, alternating flashes of red and white light. It looked pretty, sending its bright flashes over the dark waters. This morning we met a four-masted sailing vessel. The wind was sending her through the waves at a lively pace. Sailing ships look much nicer on the water than steamers, especially when they are going before a good breeze with a full head of canvas.

The ladies who were out on the deck singing the first night out from Seattle have not been heard from in like manner since. I expect they have been doing their singing in a different key the last day or two.

The accommodations on the *Centennial* are not as good as on the *City of Seattle*, but they are as good as the average, and really better than I expected. They are not as good as they were going up on the *City of Pueblo*, but I have not been nearly as sick this time, so I have enjoyed it better.

I disliked the *Dolphin* about as much as any boat I ever traveled on, but she was so overcrowded you could hardly expect good accommodations.

May 19, 1904

2 PM: Southern Pacific, Depot, San Francisco, waiting for the three o'clock train for Pacific Grove. We landed in the city last night, at half past ten. It was dark before we reached the Golden Gate, but it was a clear night and the moon was about a third full. We could see the flashes of the Farralone Island light.

All the lights about the bay were shining brightly, and looked very pretty as we came up the harbor. This morning I was walking on Market street after breakfast, when whom should I meet but R.C. Beck. I had suspected that he would be well on his way toward the South Seas by this time, but the expedition has been delayed.

Edwin Warren

ACADEMY OF SCIENCES GALAPAGOS EXPEDITION

He took me up to the Academy of Sciences and presented me to Professor Loomis, the director. The professor said that the expedition to the Galapagos Islands would only stay one year, instead of two as originally intended. He said it would probably start the middle of June and he said he wanted me to consider the proposition of going on the trip. He seemed to think it was a fine opportunity for me.

May 19, 1904

7 PM: HOME AGAIN PACIFIC GROVE, CALIFORNIA

END OF THE SECOND JOURNEY 1904

APPENDICES
The Stanford Years

1908 Stanford year Book the Quad
Courtesy of Stanford University

89

Class of 1908
Courtesy of Stanford University

EDWIN'S CLASSMATES OF 1908

ROW ONE
Vail, S.M. — Vandervoort, T. , Wallace — Miss E. — Walker, W.M.

ROW TWO
Ward, Miss H.M. — Warmont, Miss L.J. , (Edwin Victor Warren) — Wasson, Miss C.

ROW THREE
White, J.K. — Wilkins, Miss N.H. — Wilson, Miss C.E. — Wilson, Miss E.T.

ROW FOUR
Won Dries, C.H. — Wond, D.E. — Wright, Miss R.A. — Yasuda, J.K.

Edwin Warren 1908
Courtesy of Stanford University

MORE ABOUT THE AUTHOR

EDWIN WARREN, THE BIRDMAN OF TREADWELL

Edwin's parents came from Pennsylvania. His mother saw the smoke from the Battle of Gettysburg from their farm. His mother also saw Abraham Lincoln debate Douglas, and shook hands with Lincoln. The Warrens came out to California from Pennsylvania by the Iron Horse. Edwin was very interested in the sciences and most especially ornithology.

Edwin was attending Stanford during the 1906 San Francisco fire and earthquake, which I understand did extensive damage to Stanford.

Edwin never told me of his experiences at the Treadwell Mines, but fortunately he kept his diaries, much like a time capsule, preserving these experiences for everyone to experience, as if you were there yourself at the Treadwell mine underground, witnessing death and injury.

—Barry Kibler

GLOSSARY OF MINING TERMS

1. Amalgamator - The process of using mercury to attract small particles of crushed gold and join them in an amalgam alloy; the gold is recovered from the mercury and the mercury can be recovered.
2. Bedrock - Solid rock under the gravel or soil.
3. Claim - A parcel of public land a miner claims the right to mine for precious metals.
5. Gangue - Worthless rock in a vein which may hold gold.
6. Geology - Study of rocks in the earth.
7. Glory hole - A big pit where the gold was first discovered and the mining process began.
8. Gold - A soft, yellow precious metal.
9. Jigging table - A vibrating table with different-size screens, set on an incline to separate ore after passing through the stamp mill.
10. Level - Horizontal cut in a mine, usually between shafts that provide access to ore for stoping.
11. Mercury - A heavy liquid used to help separate the gold from other metals.
12. Ore - A mixture of minerals and gangue, from which gold can be extracted.
13. Sands - What remains after the ore has been processed by jigging tables.
14. Shaft - Vertical entrance to a mine cut downward from the surface.
15. Stope - Excavation created by the removal of the ore and subsequent widening of the drift.
16. Tailings - Fine particles of ore deposited as waste after processing by the stamp mill.

TREADWELL BENEFITS:

1. Housing for families.
2. Bunk houses for single miners.
3. Hospital plan.
4. Library.
5. Schoolhouse.
6. Citizenship classes.
7. Grocery store.
8. Soda fountain.
9. Playhouse.
10. Gymnasium.
11. Tennis courts.
12. Treadwell club band.
13. Natatorium (indoor pool).
14. Many more not listed.

ABOUT BARRY KIBLER

I was born in Concord, California on June 6, 1939. Just three years later, my dad died of cancer at the young age of forty and my brother and I were destined to be our own fathers. For our mother Margaret, named after Edwin's sister the missionary in Honolulu that Edwin writes to in the diaries, never remarried. Compounding this was the fact that she did not drive. Bicycles were for transportation, not toys. Our mother was a housewife and did not work, like most women in those bygone days.

Despite these hardships, we managed to grow up okay, largely due to my grandfather Edwin Warren helping us, by buying us a nice home in Berkeley, California. He lived with us there for about three years. These three years in Berkeley were the best years of our childhood. My brother and I were in the Boy Scouts and the YMCA and the Berkeley Junior Traffic Police (crossing guards). For this we were rewarded with free matinees at all three theaters in Berkeley on Saturday, and free football games where we would watch Edwin's Stanford Indians play against Berkeley's Golden Bears. This was when I got real acquainted with the man I would grow to love and respect, as I never respected anybody before or since. He never mentioned the diaries or his journeys to Alaska to me. However, I imagine that big bearskin rug that was in our living room was the one that Edwin talked about when he was talking to that old bear hunter who told him how Indians hunted bear with primitive rifles.

THE END

Made in the USA
Lexington, KY
23 September 2013